LIVING WITH
DOGS

LIVING WITH
DOGS

Tales of Love, Commitment, and Enduring Friendship

Henry and Mary Ellen Korman

Wildcat Canyon Press
A Division of Circulus Publishing Group, Inc.
Berkeley, California

Living with Dogs
Tales of Love, Commitment, and Enduring Friendship
Copyright © 1997 by Henry Korman and Mary Ellen Korman
Cover photograph © 1996 Paul Coughlin/Jim Dratfield, Petography, Inc.

PUBLISHER: Julienne Bennett
EDITOR: Roy M. Carlisle
COPYEDITOR: Marianna Cherry
COVER AND INTERIOR DESIGN: Gordon Chun Design
TYPESETTING: Holly A. Taines
TYPOGRAPHIC SPECIFICATIONS: Body text set in Minion 11/15. Chapter titles are Cosmos ExtraBold 12/15.

Printed in the United States of America
Library of Congress Cataloging-in-Publication Data
Korman, Henry, 1941–
    Living with dogs : tales of love, commitment, and enduring friendship / Henry and Mary Ellen Korman.
        p. cm.
ISBN 1-885171-19-6 (pbk. : alk. paper)
1. Dogs. 2. Dog owners. 3. Human-animal relationships. I. Korman, Mary Ellen, 1941–   . II. Title.
SF426.2.K65 1997
636.7'001'9—dc21   97-27230 CIP

Distributed to the trade by Publishers Group West
99 98 97   10 9 8 7 6 5 4 3 2 1

Contents

Thanks

To all the people, named and unnamed, who gave unsparingly of themselves, reflecting upon and giving voice to their feelings of warmth and devotion to the dogs in their lives.

To Julie Bennett whose feelings about how deeply dogs affect us were a continuing source of inspiration and a guiding beacon.

To Roy M. Carlisle for firmly and gently shepherding each and every draft of the manuscript through all the mills which grind exceedingly fine.

To Tamara Traeder, Holly A. Taines, Rose Bargmann, and Lenna Lebovich for their kind support and encouragement.

To everyone at Gordon Chun Design, especially Gordon Chun for a sensitive design, and Dana Nakagawa for a cover that sets the stage; Jim Dratfield of Petography, Inc. in New York City for a winning cover photo; and Lloyd Francis Designs in San Francisco for making the backcover photo session a treat.

Priscilla Stuckey for her thoughtful developmental review which helped every story find its proper place, Marianna Cherry for fine-tuning our words with a rigorous copyedit, Virginia Macgruder who proofread in record time, and Jeannie Trizzino for transcribing hour after hour of interview recordings.

For the great good humor of everyone at Circulus.

Our great appreciation for the constant and loving support of Vivian Hampton, Faye Mary, Janet and Wayne Forbes, and Barbara and Patrick Patterson.

To dogs everywhere, to Maggie for her sustaining enthusiasm, to the beloved dogs we've lived with, and to Chang, our venerable Chow whose growth in accepting infirmity has touched our hearts.

INTRODUCTION

Although I saw you
The day before yesterday,
And yesterday and today,
This much is true—
I want to see you tomorrow, too!

Masuhito

I own a dog? I have a dog? No. Our relationship, Dog's and mine, isn't defined in terms so precise and so limited by the formalities of possession and ownership. I live with Dog. Dog lives with me. We live together.

Living together means being present for the whole of Dog's life from beginning to end. There's the first glimpse of a breathing ball of fur no more than a handful, puppyhood and getting to know what we bring to one another, adulthood with its rhythms of work and play, old age with a slowing down and preparing to voyage on. We live together . . . and while Dog's life has always seemed shorter, ours longer, the differences in length ultimately are of little importance—each of us has an entire life to live, whole and timeless.

The whole of the life of another being fitting into a part of our own; the life of a being who lives in ways that we aspire to live in: without vanity, envy, bitterness, or pretensions; with wholeheartedness and natural joy, love, and forgiveness.

No wonder we feel expanded when we bring a dog into our lives.

The origins of our bond with dogs are hidden in the vastness of ancient prehistory. Domesticated for as long as a hundred thousand years, they have certainly been by our side since we first took refuge in caves more than twenty thousand years ago, their images incised into the surface of the stone or beautifully drawn, as if they had coalesced from the smoke of a campfire. A dog has even been found cradled in the arms of a man who had been buried circa 9,000 B.C.E., an obviously beloved being.

Over the millennia, the relationship between humans and dogs has remained remarkably constant. Dogs have guarded us, worked for us, played with us, kept us company. And, for most of this time together, people have lived in a profound and intimate union with nature. The passage of the seasons, the vagaries of weather, storm and drought, plagues of insects or microbes, daily contact with beasts of burden: all have been defining aspects of human experience.

But within living memory, for millions of people, the balance between human and dog and nature has shifted. During the nineteenth and early twentieth centuries, a large portion of the world's people went from a rural-agrarian to an urban-industrialized society, with the remainder, although lagging behind, heading in the same direction. Most recently, much of our society has become postindustrial and increasingly technology-dependent. These changes have been accompanied by a divorce from nature. Contact with nature is packaged in the form of a picnic, a skiing trip, river-rafting, a drive in the country—we go do something in a natural setting and then leave it to return home. A storm is no longer a matter of possible life and death; it's an annoying cause for the cancellation of a professional baseball game—if the stadium has no roof! Many people leave their apartments, take a subway train to work, spend the day in a windowless office, and return home having had little or no contact with anything not manufactured.

To us who live in a technologized society, dogs have taken on a new and important value: living with a dog brings the natural back into our lives. Their presence requires that we interact with a natural creature on a continuing basis. They must be loved, played with, fed, their toilet needs accommodated—not occasionally or when we're in the mood, but day in, day out. This deeper valuation of dogs is also revealed by a new willingness to spend more money caring for a sick or older dog than people would have spent in the past. It's not that in the past people haven't loved their dogs as much as we do; it's that our dogs add a dimension to our lives that formerly was taken for granted, and that otherwise would now be absent.

Compounding our separation from the natural is our tendency to live increasingly in a mental world, only fleetingly aware of our bodies or of our emotions. Television, movies, computer games, the internet, much of our work—all involve lots of thinking, the action taking place within the confines of the mental arena. The sight or sound or presence of a dog can change everything as if from black and white to color. Suddenly we're in a vivified world—a world of feeling, of sensation—a world living, breathing, and pulsating with life. Our dogs can return us to that world, introduce us again and again to the rich experience of communing with our feelings and instincts. When it comes to thinking, there's no doubt we win over dogs hands down. But they have an emotional and instinctual intelligence we too often take for granted, an emotional intelligence we hunger for as a complement to the thinking we are forced to depend upon.

We are enriched by the love and the many other qualities a dog can bring into our lives. And by accepting responsibility for the being in our physical and emotional care. What we get from them, we can give. It's a two-way street.

~

We began talking to dog people in America from coast to coast, Canada, and Australia, asking them about their experience of living with dogs. What people told us varied but was built on a shared foundation: a unique, important, loving bond with a creature of another species who wants to connect with us. Time and again, we heard people say, "My dogs have a profound effect on me. I see other people affected in the same way; I see it all the time! What is it that dogs do for us? Why do we love them?" Every one of these people had happily exchanged stories about their dogs with other dog lovers at a puppy-training class, while walking the dog in a park, or over a cup of coffee at work. We've never met any dog person who wouldn't tell their favorite story at the drop of a hat. And story always leads to story; each incident, remembered, triggers another that's just got to be told and heard. Once started, the cascade is hard to stop.

What was special for the speakers this time was turning the spotlight on themselves, focusing on how they felt and what they understood about dogs, about the situation and events they were describing—perhaps for the hundredth time. And as the people we spoke to reflected on their experience, putting what they felt into words, almost every one of them for the first time, often we heard their voices catch, or saw a light enter their eyes, sometimes tears. Complete strangers to us would bring forth their innermost thoughts, feelings, and experiences solely out of a mutual love and respect for dogs. Gradually we saw what needed to be told—the story of people who love dogs living with dogs who love them.

The mystery of this connection, and the awe which accompanies the experience of its depths, rippled through the competent, authoritative voice of Paul Scherke as he conversed with Mary Ellen on the phone one January night from Ely, Minnesota, where he owns and operates Wintergreen Lodge for recreational dog-sledding. People come from all over world each winter to spend from a few days to a few weeks getting to know firsthand these dogs who love to work in cooperation with other dogs and people. Paul has made many sledding expeditions to both poles, his first to the North

Pole in 1986. "This is my eighteenth season, sharing my home with several dozen other mammals, all of them Canadian Eskimo dogs," he mused. As the night deepened, wondrous tales of a life spent in the company of dogs at both poles of the earth slipped from the speakerphone. Paul began speaking of a five-month trek he had undertaken with a friend across North America, all the way from Minnesota to Alaska: "A large portion of the journey took place along the Beaufort Sea, on the border of the Canadian Arctic. One day, out of the white of the blowing snow, a dog appeared. At first, we were afraid it might be a wolf from the near forest, but it was a dog. Although he was very skittish and wouldn't let us get anywhere near him, he traveled along with us for the next couple of days some distance behind the sled, showing himself from time to time."

Paul and his partner were very curious about where the dog had come from and why he had suddenly appeared out of the middle of nowhere. "We attempted to coax the dog toward us and get him to nibble some food from our hands. Gradually, he became less and less fearful of us and of our dogs, until finally he gained the courage to run alongside the team. Our dogs were harnessed two by two in front of the sled, and my partner had the idea that we leave one of the spots empty to see if the dog was keen on assuming a position on the team.

"A few hours after we'd taken one of the team out of harness to leave an open slot, the dog moved in and ran in position perfectly, exactly where he would have been had he been in harness. All the days he'd been following us, he clearly had been looking us over, hoping to find a place on our team. It became apparent that the dog had, in the not too distant past, been part of a team and had run away or been abandoned. He was keen to hook up again with what he knew to be his lot in life. Once we were able to slip a harness on Sam, as we named him, he pulled on our team for the rest of our journey to Alaska. In fact, not too many days after he began pulling, we saw he was an exceptionally good and well-trained lead dog.

"He just appeared out of the mist one day on the Beaufort Sea," Paul concluded, his voice filling with wonder, affection, and pride. "He found us out there. He found something that looked familiar—men with a team of dogs—and knew that was his place."

Sam went on to become one of the first dogs in history to lead expeditions to both poles. Old at the time he found Paul thirteen years ago, Sam's now retired, a happily settled family pet.

CHAPTER ONE

A ZEST FOR LIFE

My idea of good poetry is any dog doing anything.

J. Allen Boone

A thin silvery stick twirls through the air, flashing in and out of branchy shadow, silhouetting against the scudding clouds. A bundle of energy and muscle wrapped in fur bounds across the grass, vectoring in toward an intersection with the stick hanging in space. A last gathering, a springing upward, a straining forward, and a dog plucks the stick from the air, then returns to earth. The dog trots up to a human, offering it. "Throw it again," the dog asks, in no uncertain terms. A Frisbee, a ball, a stick: Dog doesn't care about what's thrown, only about the throwing, the joyous silky flow of living the moment.

At the start of our walk with Dog, we felt a bit down, stale, and sluggish, weighted with a pack of little troubles that wouldn't be solved today or tomorrow. Now we bend to accept the stick. Back muscles stretching, we breathe out and then, as we straighten, feel the air filling our lungs. With another deep breath, we cock our arm and fling the stick high and far for the dog. As our arm drops, we notice the clouds for the first time, rich with moisture and the promise of a gentle rain.

And the trees are budding out, misting the branches with the palest of greens. Dog springs for the stick and races back with a smile. Our troubles lightened, we walk on. Life is good, again.

No shades of gray

We treasure our dogs' wholehearted acceptance of life. Their acceptance is rarely grudging, rarely passive; it is usually a simple coming forward to meet the moment with energy and interest. And so often their zest for life rubs off on us. Nancy Dusseau, a lawyer and businesswoman, put it this way: "I love my dogs greeting me at the door, jumping up and down like I'm a long lost friend. When I get a little down, they are so good-natured and so cheerful that being around them brings me back up again. It's infallible. Relationships with humans can have the same effect, but usually they carry complicated obligations with them. With dogs it's relatively simple. There are no shades of gray—you pay attention to them, give them lots of exercise, keep them healthy ... and they adore you. I can't think of anything else in the world like that."

Interacting with a dog can light up our senses, instantly. A simple glance may be enough to trigger happy feelings. "I love seeing Maggie's little shape and that happy tail," Julie, a publisher, explained about her Scottie. "My friend was playing with Maggie, who was just beside herself with joy. Her tail was wagging, her rear end was going, every inch was wiggling. There's something about the sight of her—it's like seeing someone you love, but with dogs it often seems more intense. Maybe it's because they're so pure." And that purity evokes an equally pure response.

Rather than feeling provoked and scolding him, Bonnie Hampton relied on her understanding as a psychotherapist and lightheartedly permitted Dugan to carry on with his dog's affairs. Smiling, she remembered that "Whenever my family came visiting us in winter, Dugan stole people's socks, took them out in the yard, and buried them in the snow. There the socks remained, hidden until the arrival of spring when the snow melted and I'd find them strewn all over the back yard. I'd gather them, wash them, and people would come to claim their own. It was joyous."

Diana, dogless in Vancouver, borrows her friends' dogs. It's not the doggy frolics she misses, but rather the justification they offer for her own. Diana explained that "if I ran around my backyard waving a big stick in the air or wrestled around on the floor, people would think I'm a little crazy. But if I do that with a dog, it's okay. Our society is so formal—we don't have many outlets for our energy and playfulness."

Connecting to the natural world

"You get up, go to work; you pay your bills, shop for groceries; you play with your kids, watch football on Sundays, and go to work again on Monday. You have to gas up the car—no time to watch a bluebird take off and fly across the lawn. If you do, you'll be late for work.

"This," points out Lynne Crosby, a dog behavior trainer

and breeder, "is the rhythm of much of our lives. One of the things a dog can do is help us step back, relax, and connect with the natural world." Dogs' senses complement ours; our sense of smell, for example, is weak, theirs is strong. "What is he sniffing at the base of that tree? Are there bobcats here? What marks does he see there?" If we let the intelligence of their senses inform our thinking, a hidden world can open up. "You watch the dog and think, 'The other day we saw a deer near this spot. He must be following the trail and maybe that's the way they always go. I bet if we come early in the morning we'll see them.' We begin to appreciate how the world runs on its own schedule."

Lynne believes this appreciation affects our feelings as well as our intellects. Our bond with the dog can broaden, at least for a while, to connect us to the whole of the natural world. Rather than viewing a forest as a resource, "we have and enjoy the *spirit* of the forest, so that the air breathes life into us. Dogs help open our senses because they approach being in the forest from a different perspective. They don't have the jingle-jangles. They don't have the sense of 'I have to do something else now.' They're always present—totally there. Because of our emotional connection with them, we can be there too, in a way we couldn't otherwise."

Director of quality assurance for a pre-eminent West Coast high-tech software company, Rose agrees fully. "My dog reminds me to pay attention to the everyday—to be present. Especially when everything gets filled with stress, it's great to just take her for a walk. There she is, running around being so happy. Her freedom and awareness as she runs ahead of me—sniffing the air and the earth, or chasing a leaf, or listening to the birds sing, or greeting people—are a good reminder of what life's all about."

And then there are the aspects of nature we'd rather not connect with! Halfway across the continent, Morgan Watkins runs a computer company through the University of Texas at Austin. He was looking forward to celebrating the first anniversary of his partnership with Fantom, his guide dog, when they became involved with nature quite suddenly—and a bit too intimately. "After Fantom and I got home, we zipped through the house and into the backyard, where we bounced around in the grass playing fetch. Suddenly, Fantom lost interest in his toys and ran along the fence by the side of the house. I got suspicious. He was running as though he had something better to catch. Cat? Possum? Or? . . . Then the air filled with a thick, acrid scent. Strong—not just strong—damn near overwhelming. Fantom had found a skunk no more than a few feet from me. Instantly, the two of us reeked.

"I said, 'Come on, Fantom, let's go inside.' We stink, therefore we should go in the house—right? My wife and son weren't quite sure what to do with us. I said something lame, like, 'I think we've been sprayed by a skunk.' They assumed we'd also been brain damaged—of course we'd been sprayed! Did I head back outside with Fantom and a bottle of industrial-strength shampoo? Nope. We headed upstairs to the master bathroom for the dog shampoo and a Jacuzzi-sized tub. "I shampooed that poor dog five times. Finally, Fantom began to smell like my old sweet buddy. I showered several times myself and got the stench scrubbed off. But even when I finished drying Fantom, I still smelled skunk. Finally, I figured it out: the inside of his nose had been coated with the odor, and he'd been laying on the floor, rubbing his nose and getting the scent on his front paws. I suspected he'd be fine by morning. Oh well, I told him, 'Happy Anniversary, stinky!'"

A nourishing energy

Whether from the enlivening gladness that rises in us at the sight of a frolicking dog or from the eventual lift that turns a midnight potty trudge into an invigorating starry event, our association with dogs can tap energies that would otherwise lay dormant. And dogs don't drain our energy the way some people can. Mary-Louise, an environmental cleanup consultant, came to realize that her "puppies take a lot of energy—but when you pet them, they provide energy too. They're not like people, who have been called 'psychic vampires.' I don't think a dog would know how to be one. Even the problem dogs I've had—they also gave. Even an old dog like Stanley loves playing tug of war with a sock. He'll drop a sock at my feet, then grab it and run off. He particularly likes to sneak up on me when I'm watching TV with my legs crossed—he can take the edge of my sock and pull the whole thing off before I know it!"

The San Francisco Bay Area is beautiful but can seem

big and empty for someone arriving suddenly from the Midwest after leaving a marriage behind. That was Julie's situation before Maggie came into her life. The cost of living was eight times higher than any place she had ever lived, and she knew only one person. "I was miserable. I was lonely. I hated the house I had purchased and felt trapped," Julie remembered. "I kept thinking I had made the worst mistake in my life. I wanted a dog, but I refused to have one and leave it home all day by itself while I was away at my full-time job." Julie felt that having her own business would allow her to take her dog to work. "I quit my job, started my business, and got my dog. It had a profound impact on me emotionally—my whole life changed. My little dog went to work with me and came home with me. All of a sudden I loved my house, because it was filled with the love this dog gave me. It seemed warmer, more like a real home."

When he was a young man studying biology in college, Rob worked part-time for a nursing home where he saw visiting dogs enliven patients who had lost interest in life. "The elderly people—there were about a hundred—had very few visitors. My girlfriend saw something on television about bringing animals into nursing homes to make people feel there's more to life than watching TV and smoking. She and I each had two dogs, and we gained permission to bring our pets in." The effect was spectacular. "People there went crazy over the dogs. It was unbelievable. Someone who'd been sitting doing nothing for whole days got up to pet the dogs.

And the dogs were also going crazy—they loved the attention." Since Rob's other job was at the Humane Society, he brought visitor dogs from the kennel. "The elderly people got together and actually adopted one. It really changed them—they'd shuffle up and down the hallway, but whenever the dog came running around the corner, they'd sit down and pet it."

Advanced age complicated by a serious illness is particularly draining. Diagnosed with cancer, Craig's mother had a short time left to live. She remained at home with twenty-four-hour nursing, confined more and more to her bed. During a period when she was particularly down, Craig, a former Disney Imagineer who now gives creativity seminars in corporations, thought to take his Dachshund for a visit. "My dog had never been to my mother's house. As soon as I opened the sliding glass door on the patio, Schatzi ran in, jumped onto my mother's bed, put her head on my mother's stomach, and they hit it off." Craig saw an immediate change in his mother; she sat up in bed and was much more alert. Schatzi made such a huge difference he left her for a few days with his mother, who remained alert until the last days of her life.

Debbie has had a succession of Toy Poodles nearly continuously for thirty-six years. Five years ago, when her sixteen-year-old daughter was seriously injured, she learned just how much her dogs could give. "After three months in a rehabilitation hospital, my daughter came home to recuperate before returning to school. She was paralyzed on her left side, but when she sat on the floor Coco and Bridget were all over her, so she was able to play with them. The joy and feeling of well-being they brought to her during that hard time was really important in her recovery."

Icebreakers

Walk into a roomful of strangers and no one speaks to you. Walk into the same room with a dog on a leash and you're never alone. In fact, since he already has a girlfriend, Michael often considered renting his Jack Russell Terrier, Jib, to single friends because "he's a real babe magnet. When we go to a park, women always come up to me, very friendly, wanting to talk about the dog. Some single male friends of mine have noticed this, and they've asked if they could have him for a weekend to walk him or take him to a party. When single people ask me, 'Could I meet many people with a dog?' I answer, 'As many people as you can stand to meet.'"

We tend to feel more comfortable meeting a stranger accompanied by a dog. "When you see a person walking up the street with a dog, your first thought isn't 'that person is going to rob me,' and you don't feel threatened (unless it's a threatening dog). No, your first thought is, 'what a cute dog!' usually followed by, 'what a nice person that is!' Often, people know your dog better than they know you! The street we just moved to is a big dog street; I've already learned the names of people's dogs, but not the names of the owners."

As executive director of Hilltop Arboretum in Baton

Rouge, Janet users her well-developed social skills in dealings with staff, patrons, and visitors. Nevertheless, her Basset Hound, Waldo, has helped her to get to know her neighbors. "To them, I'm not Janet," she says, echoing Michael's experience, "I'm Waldo's mother. I probably would never take any kind of initiative to meet my neighbors. Especially in the spring when more people come out on a regular basis, my long-eared social butterfly provides all the introductions needed. When neighbors visit, if they have dogs or dog tales, that's a wonderful entrée."

Julie thinks that being stopped on walks by people who wanted to meet Maggie helped her acclimatize to her new environment. She said, "A whole community of people has sprung up around my dog, a group of people that I know only because I walk Maggie. They know Maggie's name but not mine."

Ken, who lives a dual life as a psychologist and guitarist, lived for many years near a neighborhood tavern where he drank beer and hung out. "I had my dog Oso in the car one day, and I didn't want to leave him there. So I asked the owner if I could bring him in. He said sure—if Oso got along all right. The dog went around cleaning the popcorn off the floor. I'd gone to this place to have a beer for years, but didn't know anyone there—when I left that night, I knew everybody."

Not only is Morgan's guide dog Fantom a great icebreaker, but he helps conversations start off on the right foot. Morgan says, "When you're blind, people sometimes feel a little uncomfortable coming up to you. Then they want to start a conversation about a blind uncle they once had—not the way I prefer to have my conversations begin. When I used a cane, I was approached two or three times a week. Now with Fantom, I'm approached dozens of times a day—and mostly it starts out, 'Oh, what a beautiful dog!'

"There are some people who don't want guide dogs because of all the attention the dog gets. But if you're in business, as I am, you need to be approachable, and if you can't see well, that's hard for some people because all they can see is a handicap. What they see now is a guy with a dog. *That's* approachable. I've gone from being Morgan Watkins to The Guy with Fantom."

All of us have felt a happy lightness when, out on a walk, our dogs make a passerby smile. Or, when our houses or apartments seemed dead and lifeless—just too many inanimate objects—a vibrant dog has emanated an energy that filled the spaces and our lives with a presence far beyond the creature's actual size.

CHAPTER TWO

FINDING EACH OTHER

Friend is a dog's name.

Jamaican proverb

Finding a dog usually depends on chemistry, often on fate. Large or small? Short- or longhaired? Male or female? Mutt or purebred? Breeder or pound? So many questions, so many types of dogs to choose from. We conduct research to decide on the dog we want, but all too often we find one in the pound we click with, or one falls in our laps when we least expect it.

Born to the dogs

We think back, remembering our childhood homes and the people who made them livable. The adult world was "up there," on sofas and chairs and tables and counters, where the big people did things. For many of us, as small children playing on the floor happily, there was a dog. In our childhood, we and our dogs inhabited a world of the same scale where both of us were cared for by adults. We loved our dog, not knowing we were dog people.

Mary Ellen remembers the joy of her toddlers Bert and Dave at mealtimes, watching and being watched intently by their Miniature Poodle, Botticelli, his black eyes gleaming in anticipation of "floor manna." "The boys would eat fast so they could say they were full and then, laughing, let food 'fall' for their friend. Our saintly German Shepherd, Ivan, let both boys crawl all over him, peering into his mouth, offering him their toys—without a complaint. As they played near him, Ivan would fall asleep and then the children, in turn, would fall asleep lying on him, the three of them a bundle of snooze."

When Janet's daughter Susan was learning to walk, she'd stand beside their first Basset, Hans, and hold on to his collar to walk with him. "When Susan was all set, they would take off for a stroll around the back yard. When she was still in a cradle in our bedroom and would start squawking or fussing, he would go in, jump on the bed, look in that little cradle, and come back to us and in effect say, 'You know, you need to do something about this. Look into it!' And Hans was the first thing that made Susan laugh, she'd just get so tickled with him. They were definitely a twosome—very devoted to one another."

A veterinarian's daughter, Deborah Jacobs said, "We always had dogs. There's a picture of me when I was only two, holding Bessie, my Dachshund. I remember sitting with Bessie on my lap, how solid her body felt, and squirmy and alive—a certain vibration of 'dogness'. That awareness hooked me on animals, especially dogs." Like most children, Deborah never consciously thought of herself as a dog person. It's unimaginable that any child wouldn't love a furry playmate as much as we all did as children.

Until ten years ago, Pat would never have been called a dog person. He had little experience with dogs as a police officer on a SWAT team in Arizona. Then he moved to Oakland, California where he tried out for the city police department's SWAT team. "After one of my interviews, the sergeant in charge of the canine unit said 'Hey I like some of the things I heard you say. Would you be interested in being a dog handler?' Back in the Marine Corps I'd known some guys who handled dogs. I thought, gosh, who would want to drive around with a dog all night, hair floating around and stinking up the car? I told him I'd have to think about it."

But Pat's wife suggested he at least look into the idea. Pat went through the testing process and was selected. "I went out to the training site," Pat continued, "and saw this real thin, rangy dog in the back of the trainer's pickup. 'That's your dog,' they told me. I laughed—I thought it was just a mutt. My picture of a police dog was a German Shepherd, Rin Tin Tin. The trainer said, 'It's a Belgian Malinois, a herding breed from Maleine, Belgium. Very agile, fast, intelligent, and very personable.' I thought, well, heck, I'll take it for a week and then tell them it's not working out."

Things turned out a little differently than Pat expected. "When I brought Gitan home that night, my wife fell in love with him. She thought he was beautiful. I thought, God this dog is skinny. In just a couple of days, we really clicked. I've had him ever since then, for about ten years. My first impression of him was absolutely wrong; he's a great dog. I spend twenty-four hours a day with him, more time than with my family, yet he's an integral part of the family—my kids play with him, my wife takes walks with him, he goes on vacation with us. I have a great dog who's fun to have around the house."

Clearly, not all dog lovers are born as such. Some fall in with dogs by chance, or on the job, or are persuaded by the ardent campaign of a dog person. However it happens, there's no turning back.

Well-met

Is there anyone who can't remember the first encounter with the dog that would become theirs? Some instinctive connection prompted us to say, *this one is mine.* Perhaps it was the one puppy in the litter that sniffed and nibbled our finger, or the one dog at the pound with a raffish charm.

Pounds, shelters, kennels are dangerous places for dog people. Jim was going to buy his future wife Judy a Basset Hound for her birthday. She'd had two beloved Bassets previously. A friend warned him, "You don't surprise somebody with a *dog!*" so he told Judy about his planned gift. She said "No, let me call around and see if we can find one at a shelter." One shelter had a nice Basset/Lab mix that Judy wanted to have a look at. "What do you mean 'go look at it'?" Jim exclaimed. "You mean if we go there and you see this poor dog in this cage you are going to say 'I don't want this dog'? You might as well buy the dog food right now!" They went and looked at the dog. "Judy wanted to make sure Toby hadn't been abused," Jim continued, "so she raised her arm to see if the dog flinched. Toby's response was, 'Huh?' Then Judy started crying. I said 'I guess that means you don't want the dog, right?' And of course she got the dog. Toby's been a laugh a day for the last nine years."

Vincent remembered when "a friend's Golden Retriever had a litter of eleven pups. I saw them when they were two weeks old and picked one out, thinking, 'This one will be my dog and her name will be Melissa.' (I don't remember why the thought occurred to me—at the time I couldn't have a dog.) Melissa was sold to someone else. Two weeks later the owners brought her back claiming she was uncontrollable, and I said jokingly to my friend, 'I'll take her!' My friend came right back with, 'You can have her!' So I made arrangements to have a dog."

In Morgan's case, the personable Fantom was given to him by Guide Dogs for the Blind in San Rafael, California. Along with other blind and visually impaired people, Morgan spent a month learning to work with a guide dog. "The hardest part of the last week wasn't the wild schedule, but the anticipation of getting our dogs," Morgan remembered. "None of the blind folks, including myself, had ever had a guide dog. I had expressed a preference for a Golden Retriever, but said I would take whatever animal they thought best. At this particular time, I was warned, they had only one Golden.

"On a Tuesday night, the instructors finished their in-depth interviews during which we were asked about our work, lifestyle, shortcomings, et cetera. These were very important because the final selections depended on the information gathered on each of us. Everyone really wanted to do well.

"Wednesday afternoon we got our dogs. The instructors announced, in alphabetical order, the new master's name, the breed of his or her new dog, the gender, and the dog's name. It was a very tense moment. After waiting through A to V, they finally came to Morgan Watkins, Golden ... I felt so exuberant that I never heard the rest of what was said. I had gotten the only Golden Retriever in the bunch!

"One at a time, the instructors took us to meet our dogs. Several people broke into tears when they met their new eyes. I waited on the sofa until Fantom was brought in. He walked up to me, calmly put his head on my knee, and stayed put. I wrapped my arms around him and just hugged."

Whereas Morgan met his dog as the culmination of weeks of anticipation, dogs were far from the thoughts of Gard, a professor at the University of Guelph, Ontario. In the throes of a failing marriage, he was hoping for a cure. A trip with his wife to stay with a friend in New York State came to naught. But during the visit, fate brought a very shy puppy into Gard's life. "My friend's daughter had seen the dog cowering under a truck in New York City and spent a couple of hours coaxing her out. The dog was scabbed up and terrified. She seemed to have been abused by men—she was quite happy around women, but a man in boots and a cap made her totally freak out." After a week of barely coping, the daughter decided that the dog really needed to be in the country with her mom. But the mother couldn't keep the dog either. Gard felt an empathy with the dog. "I just started doing dog-like things. I got down with her on the ground, right at her level, and turned sideways to appear vulnerable. I sidled up to her and nuzzled her and did all the things a dog would do. She was overjoyed to have a buddy that understood her. Within an hour we were playing and rolling around on the floor together. That was the start of Chelsea and me."

Clearly, Gard needed Chelsea and Chelsea needed him. They developed an incredibly tight bond which matured and broadened as Gard moved on with his life, remarried, and had a child. "She's become a dog everybody relates to," Gard said. "Our teenage son plays with her, I feed her, my wife takes her out for walks. At this point she is not my dog alone because of changes in both our lives. She's a dog who loves people—and a lot of people love her."

Lee, who builds and maintains race cars, was experiencing the worst moments of his life having put his dog to sleep after fifteen and a half years. He swore he would never have another; the suffering was too great. One evening a friend, a student veterinarian interning on the night shift at a local pound, phoned him anxiously. "The night shift was when they put dogs to sleep and incinerated them," Lee explained. "This part of the job was the most cruel, most awful thing for my friend, a real animal lover. So whenever she could, she'd give an animal a little tranquilizer to knock it out, put it in the trunk of her car, and take it home to try and place it. She had seven cats and fourteen dogs in a small apartment where she wasn't supposed to have even a fish."

She told Lee she'd rescued one of seven dogs, all of them half-Akita, half-Pit Bull, that had just been confiscated from men who were training them as fighting dogs. At that time, the pound didn't place Pit Bulls or Pit Bull mixes; they put them to sleep. She asked Lee to take the dog for a day or two while she found a home for him. Lee agreed.

"When she brought him out of the car, he had a muzzle on, his head was covered with dog bites, his ears were still red on the edges from having been recently cropped," Lee remembered. "And he had this strange look—he stared right into my eyes. But he wasn't aggressive, he didn't act mean or anything. We brought him into my living room. I petted him and gave him some food, and put out a blanket and pillow in a corner. He laid down on the blanket and stared at me until I went to bed. I was a little spooked; every time I looked at him he looked directly into my eyes.

"The next morning, I made us both some breakfast and took him out. The first time he saw another dog, he bristled and became rigid, like an iron spring. I brought him back to the house for the day, left for work, and came home about six that night. I sat down in my chair and turned on the TV and he sat there and stared right at me. I thought, 'Boy, if this is going to be like last night, maybe I'll go stay in the other room.'

All of a sudden, he got up, walked over to me, put his head in my lap and pushed down really hard, communicating something very deep and intense. He was saying something like, 'Save me.' Or, 'I choose you.' At that moment, I realized this was the dog for me—I felt this instant communication that I don't think I'd ever felt with an animal.

"He was just the greatest dog," Lee said, fondly. "It took about a year and a half for him to be trained not to be aggressive to other male dogs. Within two years I never needed to put a leash on him, and he went everywhere with me for the next fifteen years. It was as if he understood that I'd saved him, and that he'd saved me from my resolution to not have any more dogs."

The hearts of dog people are always open to the appeal of a particular dog. A late night phone call, a chance meeting with a stray, a gift of a helping or a working dog—and two lives are miraculously engaged in an enduring relationship. So many factors conspire to bring us together, and we so often are brought together despite the odds, that our meetings seem more the action of a kind fate than indifferent chance.

CHAPTER THREE

LOVING COMPANIONS

'Tis sweet to hear the watch-dog's honest bark
Bay deep-mouthed welcome as we draw near home;
'Tis sweet to know there is an eye will mark
Our coming, and look brighter when we come.

Lord Byron

Companionship: the characteristic first mentioned by almost everyone when speaking about what dogs bring us. The words *companionship* and *companion* evoke the warmth of an embracing togetherness that endures through all the highs and lows of life. Dogs go where we go, live where we live, respond to our moods, engage our interest, keep us company. We call our dogs companions naturally, easily, intuitively aware of what the word means to us without knowing, perhaps, that it harkens back to the first dogs who were given food at a nomad's fire. Companion comes from the Latin: *com* meaning 'with', and *panis* meaning 'bread', to form *companio*: literally, a bread fellow, a messmate. A companion is a being who shares the food which sustains life.

Like the spokes radiating from the hub of a wheel, all the many different experiences of a dog's company connect to the universally felt quality of companionship, of sharing.

Building on the foundation of that experience we hold in common, we asked dog lovers, "What does companionship mean for you?"

Just like family

Companionship resides in the thousand ordinary little things we do with our dog every day. None of them are spectacular or unique: almost everyone experiences them. Julie spoke for a thousand others when she said, "Basically, we just live together. We're almost always together, unless I go out at night. Maggie goes to work with me in the morning and sleeps in my bed at night. She is there all the time." Julie's words begin to define what family means.

Although often visited by their two grown daughters, Wayne and Janet's household is now comprised of them, their cat, and Waldo, the current incarnation in a line of Basset Hounds. Of the animals, Janet said, "They're a part of our experience of our family. Our daughters grew up with and loved all our pets as a matter of course. Waldo retires to bed and curls up by me, and the cat by Wayne—the whole family! We've got an old bean bag as a ramp up to the bed for Waldo since he couldn't otherwise access his lounge area with his stubby legs." Reflecting on what she'd said, Janet added, "I never really saw the point in having what you would call a 'pet' if you lock him or her out in the backyard. The dogs have always been in the house, a part of our household. That's the way I grew up, and it's the way we've adopted for ourselves."

Many people set up rules about how animals should be treated. They believe there's a certain way to play with a dog, or that a dog shouldn't sleep in bed with them. As product manager for a software company that allowed dogs at work, Lisa had to make sure Blarney followed the rules. But at home, Lisa said, "As far as I'm concerned Blarney could sit on one of the chairs at the dinner table with my husband and me and that would be just fine. If I have some ice cream, I'll let Blarney have a lick. People get disgusted and ask, 'How could you put that in the dog's mouth?' I think his mouth is probably cleaner than the mouths of most people I know. It just doesn't bother me.

"Our bed for Blarney is like his doghouse. I really enjoy the bonding that takes place there. We play little games with him under the quilt—tie dog bones up in socks and bury them in the bed and make him find them. I like to snuggle a lot, have him in bed on one side of me and my husband on the other. Blarney always needs to be touching you, his body right against one of your sides. In the evening, if we watch TV in bed, Blarney's there with us—the three of us.

"My husband is usually up in the morning before I am, but Blarney likes to sleep late. When I wake up, he's lying there, either all stretched out or wrapped around me somehow. I pet him and hug him and tell him that I love him. Sometimes we'll wake up with the bed full of stuffed animals he's brought in during the night."

Cindy is a volunteer at the Indianapolis Humane Society.

She expresses what is true for many of us when she admits that, "Maxwell is spoiled rotten. He's a Dalmatian my husband gave me for my birthday, and he's so cute and I love him so much, he's all I talk about. I couldn't get through half my days without him. My sister says I'm obsessed with my dog and people tell me I need to have a baby. I already do—Maxwell." Cindy added, "Although we do want to have children, eventually, right now he is like a child, but also a best friend and a pal to me."

In hard times, families find children and grandchildren coming back to live at home after having left the roost. It's a good thing that Vivian, who lives with her husband, Gordon, in a small rural community, loves dogs because she found herself raising "granddogs" and "nephew-dogs." "Lynn moved to an apartment where she couldn't keep Casey, who then came to live with us. Liz was traveling a lot, and Lucky Dog finally didn't want to go back to apartment living after staying with us here in the country where she had so much freedom. Rusty, my next-door niece's Catahoula Hound, would knock on our door to come in for company after my niece got on the school bus." Then a Golden Retriever stray showed up and Vivian began feeding her. "I told Gordon, 'That dog is so grateful and so beautiful.' He said, 'If you have to have her, okay.'"

Dog lovers are sometimes accused of treating their dogs like children. But in at least one regard, the differences are unmistakable. Deborah, who grew up in a veterinarian's household and is now a mother of three, elaborates: "Our kids will grow up, become independent individuals, and go off on their own. But the dog is not going anywhere. That's taken me a long while to absorb—although on some level I've known she'll spend her whole life with me. Even though it's a shorter lifetime than I'd like, that's how it is."

As manager of training in a large software company, Barbara knows people well. She says that her dog "really is a like a person, with her own with feelings, needs, and wants. Katie knows what I'm feeling. If I've had a bad day she climbs up on the bed and licks me on the face, as if telling me everything's okay. It's similar to my knowing she's worried about a stranger at the front door, and reaching down to reassure her." Barbara also finds that talking out loud helps her sort out her thoughts. "Katie is a good listener and, unlike humans, she never interrupts!"

Everywhere we go, dog goes too

A human out walking a dog is a commonplace sight. So is a dog sunning on a front porch or frolicking with children through the lawn sprinklers on a summer day. Where is Dog the rest of the time? Safely tucked away out of sight and mind in a doghouse? Not necessarily. For most of their lives, dogs are portable. Pups are small enough to pick up and carry; adult dogs locomote themselves. Even elderly dogs can have the pleasure of making the rounds with us if we accommodate ourselves to their pace. Dogs accompany us hiking, swimming, camping; in hotels, motels, and restaurants; in cars, trucks, planes, four-wheel all-terrain vehicles, boats, and canoes. Wherever we go, Dog can go too.

Ken, a psychologist who also finds time to play guitar in a band, enjoys the company of his and his neighbor's dogs, on good days and bad. "In fact, if it's not a good day, I'll say, 'Let's go to Mount Tamalpais, I found a nice trail.' We go there—my dog trio or quartet, depending on how many sign up. I may be having the worst day in my life, but if I go out on a five- or six-mile walk with the dogs, I feel great. I'm blessed because I give my time to the dogs."

Gard takes Chelsea canoeing to add to the pleasures of hiking with the dog. "In a canoe, you can sit and look around or lie there and soak up the heat and sun." However, "in a boat you want a dog to be responsible, because you can't have the dog tipping the thing over. But Chelsea was always responsible."

When he's not hunting with his two black Labradors, Hal, a photographer, hikes and swims with them. "I live right on the San Francisco Bay and Reilly and Quinn swim out with me stroke for stroke. If I turn left, they turn left—kind of a water ballet. All the neighbors love to see the dogs swim with me."

Then there are those times when we pack our duds, get in the car, and hit the road for some adventure farther afield. Dogs make great traveling companions, never arguing or disagreeing about which road to take or what sights to see. Nancy, with her background in law, is an adventurous person who likes a challenge. She accepts not just the feeling of security her traveling companion offers, but also the spice of the unexpected. She had heard tall tales about the difficulties of traveling with dogs in another country, particularly south of the border. "Honestly, any woman traveling by herself in Mexico should take a dog. It just makes it so much easier. People seem to focus on the dog and not on the fact that you're a woman traveling alone. My dogs were like my little buffer zone. They gave me a few more minutes to reflect on a situation while I sized people up—were they friendly with the dogs or not? In that extra minute I could take a deep breath and decide if I felt okay and wanted to stay, or unsure and leave."

Catherine and Adam often wonder "what we did before we had a dog. Our whole schedule, priorities, and way of life have changed. We do everything together. Kaya goes to work, on vacation, to the store, rollerblading in the park—with one or both of us. About the only place we don't take her is to the movies. Having her has changed our habits. If Kaya can't go somewhere with us, we give it a second thought—do we really need to go there, do that?"

Even taking her dog to the movies presented no problem for Lisa. "We go to the drive-in rather than the regular movie theater so Blarney can come along. We flip down the back seat of our Explorer, get out the comforter, and crawl in. When we go out to dinner he'd rather come along and stay in the car than remain home." Lisa adds, "I've often been with Blarney twenty-four hours a day, including a fifty-five-mile commute each way to work. I can probably count on my fingers how many hours he's not with one of us. Nick and I each have a strong individual relationship with him, but Blarney's always happiest when the three of us are together." Recently, Lisa left her job at the company that allows dogs at work for a job at a company that doesn't. She has been concerned about the difficulties Blarney will have, so her husband will telecommute from his home office two days a week to be with Blarney to ease the transition for him.

Not only do guide dogs escort their masters to work, as Blarney accompanied Lisa, but they themselves are working and go everywhere their masters go—twenty-four hours a day, seven days a week, 365 days a year. Morgan said, "Fantom and I are a very tight pair. In the year and a half I've had him I've been away from him for a total of ten hours. He's not only my guide, he's a very close personal friend. We are partners. When we work, we merge into a singularity."

The most important thing in their relationship is trust. "I cannot move forward without his conscious concentration and attentiveness. He sees and leads; I direct and praise." Fantom gets to experience the human world by accompanying Morgan. "I expose him to a world that most dogs never experience. He goes with me into restaurants, airports, and shopping malls. When we're really cooking, Fantom is proud that he goes anywhere and everywhere and has the experience of being wherever I could be. So, he gets the attention, he gets to enjoy the nice carpeting and all the perks of being human that other dogs just don't get."

In many European countries people have a more tolerant attitude toward dogs who accompany their owners into public places than do people in the U.S. "I've lived in Europe now and again and had my dog with me," Ken reminisced. "In Spain, I took him with me to good restaurants and wrapped his leash around the foot of my chair, and he'd lie down next to me. I have pictures of him on the Metro, the Paris subway. I took him to the Galerie Lafayette, a large, fancy department store there. Taxi drivers had their dogs sitting next to them in the front seat." In the U.S., only people with guide or assistance dogs enjoy the privileges ordinary dog owners have in other countries.

Childhood pals

It's summertime, and all the other kids have gone off to camp. Nothing to do, no one to play with. Except Dog. Many of us would have felt the sting of being alone all the more sharply without the dog who kept us company. Rob summed it up for so many of us: "It was great having the companionship of a dog as a boy. When my friends weren't around I always had the dog to play catch with or ride my bike with him running beside me. Maybe that's Norman Rockwell-ish, but it's true and I couldn't think of growing up any differently."

Is there anyone who had a childhood dog who hasn't had a conspirator, as well, sometimes willing, sometimes not?

Some friends were visiting Lynn Vaughan with their little girl, Zoë, who was about four and loved Lynn's dog Maggie, a sweet, yellow Lab mix. "We were all sitting in the living room talking when suddenly I realized Maggie was missing—and that Zoë was missing, too. We looked all over, thinking they'd gone outside. Finally, I found them in a room where Zoë had taken Maggie, her water bowl, a comb, and a towel. She was giving Maggie a bath. The look on Maggie's face was a mix of terror and 'what do I do now?' Of course, it's become an institution. Now Maggie expects it and thinks it's great fun. Every time Zoë comes over, she hooks her finger around Maggie's collar and they sneak off together for their special time."

When Lee's son Christopher was born, his dog Nick immediately adopted Christopher. After bringing the baby home, Lee let Nick into Christopher's room for the first time. "I opened the door," he said, "and Nick ran directly over to the bassinet, sniffed it a couple of times, looked in, and then lay down underneath. He was instantly on guard. From then on he always watched Christopher closely. As a baby, even if Christopher poked Nick in the eye, the dog might growl at him but never bit. Often, I found them on the sofa, Nick curled in a C around Christopher who was sound asleep against him." Even though Christopher was major competition, Nick began caring for him immediately. It's likely he recognized a future pal when he saw one.

And there are the patient dogs who wait outside, kept

there by adults who don't want them in the house. David remembers his dad confining his hunting dogs to an outdoor shed, even on subzero Connecticut nights. "To some people dogs are serviceable, utilitarian things you don't let in the house. Give them a pat on the head and their food, that's it." But David wanted a more intimate relationship with their dogs. "Once, when I was nine or ten, we were spending the summer at my uncle's place. There was a thunder storm and Ranger was so nervous he came upstairs and stayed in my bedroom. That was the most wonderful thing in the world; I couldn't imagine anything better. I would have liked Ranger to come to my room back at our house, but Dad wouldn't let me. So I went out and sat with the dog in the kennel."

Warm comfort

Bonnie, who as a psychotherapist comes to grips with the intensity of human feeling every day, takes pleasure from the contrasts in the personalities of her two dogs. She offers one of the simplest, most moving reasons for keeping company with dogs: "My husband Gary travels a lot, and I needed another heart beating in the house. At first I thought I would get a big dog because my husband likes big dogs. But I'm the one who would be caring for it, so I got a Scottie, Duke. He was the weirdest little dog you've ever seen in your life—an absolute Scorpio. His birthday is in November and he's a one-person dog. He's polite to Gary, but if Gary calls him, Duke looks to me first for an okay. I couldn't tolerate Duke's being lonely while I was away from home, so I got Lucy, a West Highland terrier."

It's clear to dog people that dogs enjoy human company, that they get something from the relationship beyond being cared for physically. Bonnie went on to say, "Duke is willing to be there for me unconditionally—with his beautiful dark eyes and little wagging tail—asking nothing in return. He doesn't need to be in my lap, he doesn't need extra goodies. We have an understanding that he is absolutely fabulous and he isn't needy at all. He's delighted by large family gatherings and likes to sit at the top of the steps and greet everybody as they come up. We had two new babies in the family last year and he gets very close to sniff, but he never touches them with his nose or licks. It's so charming. He just sits and watches to discover what his role can be."

Dogs are especially welcome companions in the arctic world of snow and sledding. The Arctic Ocean, Paul said, reflecting on his treks to the North Pole, "is five million square miles of ever-drifting sea ice, an environment as vast and expansive as any on earth. Yet in many ways your world is limited to you and your dogs. Sometimes they're the only warm beating hearts within thousands of miles. It's as near as I can imagine what it must feel like to be in outer space— floating across an arctic landscape in a bath of milky whiteness with no real sense of up or down, in a little life capsule surrounding you, the team of dogs and the sled. They're your lifeline, your survival link; they're what separate you from eternity. The dogs are sources of warmth and life in what would otherwise be a very lonely experience." Remarkably, an image nearly identical to Bonnie's, that of a dog's beating heart, expressed most clearly what he felt.

Touched by our dogs, we also love to touch them. Julie says, "Touch is really important to me. We live in a society where we're not allowed to touch freely—but it's okay to touch your dog. When people feel down at the office, they pet my dog and they feel better. That's important to me. Sometimes, just having Maggie's warm body lying next to me on the couch while I'm reading or watching a movie is all I need." Dogs gladly accept our touch, and most people think nothing of our petting and touching them.

Lynn Vaughan, a licensed massage therapist, does bodywork with animals, touching them to facilitate healing. She tells of another commonly experienced aspect of ease in companionship: "In many ways it's easier to have relationships with animals—they're much less complicated than people. Animals are so straightforward. They may have their 'agendas,' but not the kinds of agendas that people have."

"As opposed to human friends," adds Angie, who lives in Vancouver with her husband Allan, their three children, a Standard Poodle, and a Bichon, "dogs maintain a constant mood toward you, whether you're upset, depressed, or sick. There's only so much you can lay on human friends, because they've got their own lives to cope with. But the dog is always there no matter what or for how long a problem persists."

James enjoys "just sitting around and seeing the little bitty things dogs do. It seems like there are a lot of human qualities in a dog that want to come out." He liked to watch his old dog Webster, who was close to ninety pounds, climb into the lap of his petite wife Johnnie and fall asleep. Sooner or later she'd have to get something and James would hear her say, "You got to get up, Web." And the dog would look at her as if to say, "Now?" She'd answer, "Yeah—you got to go." James' and Johnnie's easygoing relationship encompassed their dogs in a warm extended "conversation."

Jan is a San Francisco movie critic who as a child threw everything but stuffed dogs out of her crib. Her love of dogs continued into adulthood, helping her realize what troubles her about contemporary civilization. "I love dogs because they are totally grateful. We live in an often thankless culture that pretty much beats us up physically and mentally every day. Some dogs, like Goldens, are very grateful for everything you do for them. The pleasure they give is immediate. I'll think, 'That dog is so grateful—I must be a terrifically good person.' There's nothing like hugging a dog."

They love us unconditionally

The cliché is powerful and ubiquitous: nearly everyone uses the phrase "unconditional love" when putting into words what we find so attractive about dogs. But do dogs really love us without conditions? If we mistreat a dog, it may avoid our company; pressed, it may become aggressive, or run away.

So the dog's "love" does have a condition: a certain level of decent treatment. But given that, dogs respond with all their love. "What you give comes back two hundred times," says Debbie. "All they want is for you to pet and love them, and that's not hard to do." Dogs are sincere and uncalculating; they have no hidden agendas and are not hypocritical; they are forgiving in that they bear no grudges for a reprimand. They consistently act on their instincts and feelings without reserve and without premeditation. "Any time there's a crisis in our family, it seems as though the dog is the one steady factor," Debbie added. "They're always the same, always a warm something to snuggle. Until the day I'm no longer able to get out and walk and really take care of a dog, I will always have one."

In one way or another, dogs have been an integral part of Mary-Louise's relationships with her sister, brother, father, best friend, and ex-husband. The constancy of her dog Stanley's love has enabled her to see her own inconstancy. "I've been worse with Stanley than with any human," Mary-Louise confessed. "If something wasn't working—like my marriage—the dog was the target. I would express my anger at him. I always considered myself a very kind person, and yet here was a contradiction—if I'm so kind, how could I speak sharply to my dog just because he's sleeping in the hall-way and in a hurry I have to go around him?

"When I was angry, Stanley gave me a wide berth. He had a way of being that told me he'd be so willing to talk to me if I were kind. Taking out my irritation on the dog by my tone of voice, or pushing him out of the way, or telling him to go away when he comes up for pets left an unpleasant residue in me until I apologized and allowed myself to be forgiven by the dog. I petted and talked to him and he accepted the apology.

"As he's gotten older, I've become far more tolerant of him. I don't chastise him the way I used to. I see his kindness and his desire to be loved by me." The absence of criticism opens up an intense emotional connection that dog people find incomparable with anything else. Dogs are so accepting that they put us at ease about what we do.

The signs of a dog's love are never hard to find. When Eileen gets home from working with dogs all day at her grooming salon, "Dickens, Chewie, and Grant are all right there at the door. Dickens says, 'Okay, quick pick me up, I need a hug.' Grant stands on the sofa waiting to lick my face after I'm through the door. The minute I sit down, Dickens is in my lap and Chewie is at my feet. There's never a time I walk in the door that they're not there to greet me and that they don't seem genuinely happy to see me. It never fails."

Floyd, a stray and former sled dog, found a home with Nisa in the Yukon. The signs of Floyd's love are highly visible. "When he sees the car come up the driveway he gets excited and hops up and down and runs around and around in circles. When I pet him, he leans against me and sort of rubs his head on me. You can tell he's in ecstasy. He's got a really curly tail, and after I've been with him for a while it straightens out behind him—he's thoroughly relaxed and happy.

Freddi, a Scottie breeder, laughs off her dog's 'sign' of love. "Scotties are very independent dogs. The puppy I have now is always chewing on things. He's chewed up at least twenty socks of mine. But I don't really get mad at him or at any of my dogs. I love them enough that I can get upset with them and scold them, but I still love them and I'm sure that comes through. One of these days I'll have to go through and see if he's chewed up any pairs."

Even more than his tireless hard work, Fantom's unselfish love is what captures Morgan's heart. "His love isn't contingent upon my success as a computer guy, or as a manager, or as a family person. Fantom couldn't care less if I swing an important deal or screw something up. All I have to do is love him and he loves in return. And his love is consistent. You don't hear, 'I've had a bad day, get out of my face.' What a neat thing!—an entity whose desire in life is to be at your side without asking for anything but your attention and love. And that's the easiest to give because he earns it over and over again. I praise him and give him confidence. I brush him, clean him, feed him, and love him. He works hard for me. I do the same for him."

Honey, an international dog show judge, has been breeding English Setters for the last thirty years. "They are a gift to me. Their undaunting affection, their unlimited love. They are there when I need to be peaceful or when I need to have some fun. They'll do whatever they can for me at any time night or day and never stop to ask why.

"I love grooming them, having ten of them sitting there waiting, just for me. 'Oh great, we're getting brushed. I'm first, me, me, me!' It's wonderful knowing what they like, and that they appreciate everything I'm doing. Usually they put their head on my shoulder and bury it right into my neck. When I go down their back with the brush, like a big scratch, they just quiver, 'don't stop, that feels good, that's the spot!' It's like they've died and gone to heaven. When I stop, it's 'Aww, are we done?' I'm in tune with them and they're in tune with me."

A practitioner of non-verbal communication with people and animals, Deborah Jones has worked with dogs, cats, horses, birds, skunks, snakes—even a tarantula and a crab. She feels that all animals have something to teach us— if we listen to them. "Each one is special—you tap into different things in yourself and in them, which gives you a depth of experience. Dogs often relate by means of their body—physical contact, buddying, play. They almost force you to be intimate physically. They have so much joy and expression of pleasure that it's very easy to fall into sync with them. More than anything else I've gotten from them is the teaching of joy and unconditional love. Their underlying joy comes through."

Morgan summed up for all of us what lies at the bottom of our experience of Dog's love and our own: "His generosity, simple nature, and loyalty. I love the warmth—every single time I reach over the edge of my bed at night and find him next to me; every time I hear him snore; every time I see the way he shares his love with my wife and son, I am enriched by his presence."

Have we been anthropomorphizing the dog, mistakenly attributing human motives to an animal? Perhaps so, but this is not so foolish if considering dogs as almost human becomes a means of breaking out of the isolating mindset in which we believe we are the masters of the world. For, as much as humans aspire to unconditional love, the fact is that generally what most of us offer—and get—is love with strings attached. Receiving the unconditional kind from our dogs is a wonderful, life-affirming experience.

CHAPTER FOUR

THE TWO-SPECIES HOUSEHOLD

For it is in giving that we receive.

St. Francis of Assisi

Bearing gifts of companionship, loving acceptance, and joyful spontaneity, dogs gain a place in our hearts, and we reciprocate by planning our lives to accommodate the everyday particulars of our relationship. Since no two dogs—nor people—have identical backgrounds, experiences, abilities, or temperaments, the living arrangements we make with our dogs are varied. Some people wouldn't dream of allowing a dog to sleep in their beds, while others wouldn't be without one. Many of us train our dogs, while others happily accommodate ourselves to a dog's preferences.

No matter how much we think dogs are like us, we remember, when we see them happily poking their noses through a pile of garbage, that they are a different species, one with their own needs. Taking a dog into our homes means thinking from their point of view—and for the long term.

What we do for our dogs

All of us who live with a dog feel we get something from the association. What do we do in return? Even if we have a yard, we need to exercise our dogs. Day in and day out, dog walking is a basic, bottom-line fact of life. We grudgingly accept the necessity, wait for the last drop of rain to fall, wait until the absolute last possible moment before the doggy squirt-down—or we put aside our comfort for the dog's well-being and enjoyment.

Even in the Yukon, with much open space, a dog must be walked. "When we first got Floyd," Nisa said, "we built a big pen for him to stay in while we were at work. When we came home we'd take him for a good long walk—it didn't matter if it was forty below or the middle of the night. Floyd had to get his walk because he's a high-energy dog."

None of us wants our dog to feel lonely. When her thirteen-year-old Tibetan Terrier, Ozzie, was younger, Harriet, a public health nurse, worked all day and had no choice but to leave him alone in her apartment. "He was okay until about three thirty P.M. when he'd start 'chanting and singing,' disturbing the neighbors. My answering machine had an intercom so I'd call from work to hear if he was barking. If he was, I'd call back and talk to him during the message recording, tell him to stop barking, talk about what we were going to do that evening, saying his name often. 'Ozzie, what have you been doing? Ozzie, we'll walk down to the track tonight.' Sometimes I called back every ten or fifteen minutes to reassure him. The neighbors told me he stopped barking."

Weekends, when Lisa and Nick are taking a break from the high-tech world they work in, they'll ask one another, "What are going to do for Blarney?" They're experts at taking the dog's point of view when they choose their gift. "One Christmas day on a hike," Lisa remembered, "Blarney rolled in mud and cow manure. All we said was, 'Merry Christmas Blarney.' We knew he was in seventh heaven." What dog could ask for more?

Considering your dog's welfare in emergency situations is also part of good planning. In shake-prone California, Lisa and her husband have earthquake kits in their cars, as do many people. But they also "have one for the dog, with his food and pills and toys and water." And in case anything happens to them when traveling overseas, "we have a home already prearranged for Blarney. We picked out a family that he'd live with so there'd be no question what would happen to him if we were killed."

Inevitably, when you own a dog, you come to realize they cost money—whether in health or illness, the vet bills must be paid, and emergencies have a way of happening. Mustering great discipline, Natasa established a dog budget and a fund for emergencies. "You have to foresee things you might have to spend money on. I think I would exhaust every possible way—borrow money from my parents or relatives or friends—just to give the dog a chance."

Ed and his wife Elaine live with Teddy, a cranky Lhasa Apso, and Woody, a something or other, who with his fun charmed Ed's formerly dogless heart. Reflecting upon how much we do for our dogs, Ed says, "I've always been amazed at the expression, 'It's a dog's life.' Our dogs live in a beautiful house, right on the water, in Bel Marin Keys, and they get people to scratch their belly all the time. Yeah, a tough life. Give them the briefcase. Give them an airplane ticket. I'd trade for what they do any day."

Upping the ante

A dog can come to mean so much to us that we'll gladly do almost anything to keep it healthy and happy. We make "a few little changes" and only later do we see how much we've invested in their welfare. Mary Beth lives in the historic Garden District of New Orleans in an old house, one side of which is filled with beautiful antique furnishings. And the other side? "I have a duplex—one side is for company, the other for my two Dobermans. They've got their own living room and dining room, with a beat-up couch and rugs that they've eaten up in various parts. They've got their doggie door and they come in from the backyard with muddy feet, so it's always a mess in there. I just learned to roll with it. I had a king-sized bed where they slept with me. I didn't like that so I got them a single bed and put it next to mine, but they just wouldn't sleep in it. So then I started using the single bed and all three of us slept there. I decided to give away the king-sized bed and get them a rug to sleep on next to me. Wrong! We were all back in the single bed. Finally, I gave away the single, got a new double, and now we all sleep in that." When Mary Beth brings a visitor to the dog's side of the house, she explains simply that given Mary Beth's temperament, she felt she had either to give the dogs away or adapt to them. "I think I add to their life and they add to mine and everybody's happy." Mary Beth has a sense of humor that's as innate as her proclivity to give in to her dogs' whims. For her, ease and affection are much more important than being in complete control.

Responsibility

Most dog people develop a deeper understanding of their responsibilities during the course of their involvement with their dogs. Many of them remember a time when they weren't as responsible, when they hadn't any notion that they ought to be responsible for a particular behavior.

When Ed was a child, his family had a fenced in yard, "but the dogs could jump over it. In the summer, the tar on the streets would get warm and soft, and Pierre would lay on it—I guess it felt good on his belly—in the middle of the street. Cars drove by, honking their horns but he just looked at them as if to say, 'Who the hell are you? I'm laying here.' We'd hear the honking, but we were unaware." His wife Elaine had a similar experience as a child. "We never kept our dogs on leashes in my family, either. Freckles ran wild all day. Our neighbor would put his sneakers out on the porch to dry, and sure enough, Freckles would grab one and run. He'd follow me to school, then I'd see him at the shopping center—he was everywhere. It was amazing he wasn't killed. I didn't realize how irresponsible I was. My obedience school teacher used to say, 'A loose dog is a dead dog.' It's just a matter of time before they're hit."

Stacey O'Hara, who supervises guide dog trainers, grew up in "an average American family. We got the family Golden Retriever when I was seven. Our good friends had another Golden, a male with papers, so we decided to breed them," she said. "We got to see the miracle of birth and all, but I cringe when I remember it because it was an irresponsible way to go about having puppies. We didn't look at any of the things that ought to be screened first, such as pedigrees or histories of diseases. We did it just because the two dogs had papers, not for the betterment of the breed. It also would have been nice to have gotten a list of prospective buyers before the litter arrived, or have had the foresight not to sell the puppies without spay or neuter contracts."

Freddi, who raises Scotties, speaks for many breeders when she declared, "Any responsible breeder tries to do the very best for their breed of dog. If you breed, you are responsible for the health and welfare of each puppy until it's in a good and loving home. For me, this means taking a puppy back if the placement doesn't work out. Breeders have to reconcile themselves to the fact that this is an expensive hobby. They must part with—sell!—the puppies, not to make money but to break even or recover part of the expense. Having my puppies go to good homes overrides the pain of parting with them. I'm very emotionally involved with every one of them."

When talking with prospective families about getting a puppy, Stacey has become less enthusiastic than she used to be. "When people showed an interest in dogs, I used to get excited and urge them on. Now I'm more reserved; I stress the responsibility. People will get a cute puppy but then won't invest time in it. If you think about it, that owner will spend much more time dealing with *problems* the dog creates. All the work you put in a puppy during their juvenile years pays off big time later. I did obedience work with Sara, so she knew a lot of hand signals. That became invaluable when she got older and couldn't hear very well."

Stacey concluded, "If I can get across to another person the element of self-control for their dog and cleaning up after their dog—having a baggy with them—I feel like I've made the world a better place. If dogs are well-behaved and parks and pathways aren't littered with dog waste, dogs will be viewed more often as a public good than as a public bad." All dogs have the capacity to learn control, but not all dog owners have the desire to teach it. Lots of us let a romantic notion of "dogs being dogs" interfere with teaching them what they need to be good "citizens."

Dogs aren't toys

What are a dog's responsibilities toward children? What are our children's responsibilities toward dogs? These are often touchy subjects, yet some incidents are clear. "I've seen kids teasing or being mean to a dog, like hitting it with a stick," Barbara said, speaking for most of us. As manager of training in a software company, she has a professional's interest in the skills people acquire, or fail to acquire, not only on the job but in their lives with dogs. "I've gone and taken the dog away from the children and told them what they were doing was wrong, and brought the children to the parents." Many people believe a dog should never bite, regardless of the provocation. Barbara sees things differently. "Parents get mad at a dog for biting a child that was teasing it, but that's wrong. The dog has a right to protect itself. The kid needs to learn respect for the animal."

Some people think children should be able to pull and poke a dog. Gard said of his dog, Chelsea, "She runs from them if she can, but if she's cornered, or it keeps going on, she'll turn around and snap—but she never bites. I thought I was going to have a big fight with the next door neighbors when Chelsea snapped at one of their children. But the next day, the kids were out there playing with the dog and everything was back to normal. The kids learned that you don't yank on the dog's tail, because the dog gets pissed off. Although she wasn't going to bite them, she let them know they overstepped the bounds." And the parents needed to know that Chelsea's snapping was how dogs normally discipline and teach their puppies.

We don't want small children hurt by the dogs around them, so we should make sure the dog won't respond to children's unpredictable "touches" by nipping or biting. Nor do we want the dog ostracized as the result of a bite. To avoid these situations, Deborah Jacobs took her dog Lady to a puppy training class. "I put her through a lot in the class: pulling her tail or her ears, being unpredictable myself, and scolding if she did anything other than move away. Though I think it was tough, she did great and was a wonderful dog with the kids." Having a clear set of requirements for Lady, Deborah was equally clear about requirements for her children and their friends. "It was very important that the kids treat Lady with respect and gentleness, too. It was not okay for the kids to pull her tail or otherwise mistreat her."

When the household must change for the impending arrival of a baby, dogs can be prepared for it. Frank and Robin stopped letting their dogs on their bed. "We've gotten them out of habits that might not be good with a small child around. With some of our friends, whose dogs used to practically be the center of their universe, I've seen the entire relationship change. This is our first child, so we're looking to see what we can do so the dogs don't suffer."

Who's the boss?

When Patch came into Adam's family from the pound, he was two years old and larger than Adam's five-year-old daughter Jane. Patch assumed a position above her in the household hierarchy. "If we were paying attention to Jane," Adam remembered, "Patch would come up, swing his hips around, and give her a hockey check with his rump." To change Patch's perception of the pecking order, Adam put Jane in charge of feeding him. "We had him lie down while Jane put food in the bowl to keep him from knocking her down to get at it. It was scary for her, so we taught him to lie down several feet away from his food bowl, and to stay there until he received the release command." It took only a few weeks for the pecking order to change. "They both learned from it," Adam concluded. "She became less afraid of him and developed a more in-charge attitude, and he became more deferential toward her."

Four pushy Kerry Terriers need to have set boundaries for them. Nancy Han, a professional dog groomer married to a veterinarian, knows how. "They don't get to do things without working for it. For instance, when we feed them, they all sit, waiting while we put food in their dishes. We let my poodle and one of my little girl Kerries sleep with us. But my other Kerry can't, even though he's my favorite. When he was a puppy, we invited him on the bed, and he peed all over my husband, trying to take his position. So he got corrected and we occasionally invite him up, but he doesn't stay for long."

Sara, the Flat-Coated Retriever who accompanied Stacey through college, in her career training guide dogs, and then marriage, was also very strong-willed. "Sometimes we were like two sisters going at it. Any clash of wills was actually a lack of clear communication between us. For instance, I used to release her from a sit with the command 'okay.' Now I use 'all clear,' because once, when I had Sara sitting while I was talking to my husband Andrew, I said, 'Yeah okay' to Andrew and Sara took off. I got upset, but Andrew reminded me that I had said 'okay.'"

We ought to remember that our dogs want to please us,

even when they're doing something we might think is bad. When Nisa calls Floyd he sometimes turns and runs in the opposite direction. "He looks back as though he's thinking, 'Oh, I'd love to go to you, but I really, really have to go in the other direction.' It's not like a cat, who would just turn around and think, 'Oh, piss off, there's no way I would go to you.' Cats are aloof and independent; a dog is independent, but he is independent despite himself."

Patrice and Dawn work for a software development company and live with two Malamutes, Trey and Kayla. "If Kayla gets way out of hand," Patrice explained, "all I need to do is make her look away from me. If she keeps staring at me, we're on an equal plane, but if she looks away then I've won. Sometimes it takes a while. When she was a puppy I read the books and I followed the instructions. So, there I was, on top of her looking very mean, and telling her that Oakley sunglasses are $150 a pair and never to chew on them again. While we're staring at each other, Dawn comes in and asks, 'What are you doing?' I said to her, 'It says on page eighty-seven, I have to make Kayla break the stare.' Dawn said, 'Patrice, I don't think Kayla read the same book.'"

Nancy Dusseau likes having her dogs accompany her wherever possible. "One reason I insist that my dogs obey me and be well-trained is so I can take them more places. If they lie down quietly and don't jump on your friend's furniture or steal the kid's toys, if they're not under the table when you're having dinner, then your friends aren't going to mind having them come over. If your dogs come and raise hell, then of course people won't want them around. That was really true in Mexico. I took them everywhere with me—they can go into stores and restaurants down there, as long as they'll sit under your table."

Janet's husband Wayne maintains that the only reason they got a queen-sized bed was so their Basset Waldo would not be uncomfortable in the bed with them. "I don't know whether we latched onto Basset Hounds because they were so ugly they were cute," mused Janet, "or because they had this wonderful disposition. The Bassets we've owned had one similarity: *they* did fine in obedience school, while *I* flunked. Waldo definitely rules the roost. He may not rule anybody else's roost in the family but he definitely rules mine. Which I don't object to. I think it's nice to have someone devoted to you." And if she thinks of herself as having submitted obediently to Waldo, Janet declares, "I'm passing with flying colors. I'd get a blue ribbon every time: I take good care of my hair, I don't have any fleas, keep my ears clean, don't shed. I'm doing great. If he could talk I know he'd say he was very proud of me."

Awkward moments

Since dogs and humans do belong to different species, we don't automatically understand one another's communications. It takes time and experience to smooth out the kinks. Patrice and Dawn lived with one Malamute, Trey, then added a second, Kayla. Patrice had always had small dogs, never a big one. She was tentative, very unsure of herself with Trey. "When we were showing him," Dawn said, "I'd ask Patrice to hold Trey and she'd turn sheet white." With so many other dogs around, Patrice feared that he might turn into an aggressive, savage beast. "Trey sort of grumbles when he talks," Patrice explained. "I hadn't spent much time around the breed, so I couldn't tell an 'I'm going to kill you' growl from an 'I'm really upset with you' growl."

Dawn began a period of business-related traveling during which Patrice had to care for the dog. She began watching Trey, trying to figure him out—and playing with him. "Very quickly, he started to trust me," Patrice realized. "He hadn't trusted me before because he felt the vibes coming off me. And I trusted him, too." Patrice saw that Trey was actually very shy and non-confrontational. When people stared at him, leading him to believe he was being challenged, he'd turn his head away to avoid the confrontation. Patrice had misinterpreted his behavior. "He'd do his little 'I want to be alone' sound, not growling. But I'd never heard that sound and it was intimidating."

Another misunderstanding stemmed from Trey's size— he's smaller than many Malamutes. When a bigger dog approaches, he'll stand as tall as he can and the fur on his back stands on end to make him seem even bigger. "I thought he was getting ready to pounce," Patrice admitted. "All he's really trying to do is be as tall as everyone else because he's just a little guy. I'd had the attitude that big dogs were trouble, but they're not. And my Malamute, Kayla, has certainly blown the stereotype of any big dog that I've ever seen; she is just a gust of love."

Another type of predicament can arise because dogs don't know that not everything with a captivating odor will be good for them to eat. Cindy's Dalmatian, Maxwell, gorges on what he shouldn't. "Maxwell ate the Easter candy my mother-in-law had gotten for her grandchildren—twenty-two marshmallow eggs covered in chocolate. I was crying and calling animal control because chocolate is lethal to dogs. Fortunately, the eggs had very little chocolate and Maxwell was okay. Believe me, I'm on a first name basis with animal control: he's eaten half a pan of brownies, a loaf of garlic bread, a stick of butter with the wrapper, my husband's baseball signed by Pete Rose (oops), and frozen salmon. He also likes to chew on my shoes. Ughh. That makes me so mad! I hit him once and screamed at him. I felt terrible! But I don't get mad anymore—I just put my shoes away."

Awkward situations can be held to the minimum if we realize we may be interpreting what the dog does from a human point of view rather than the dog's. That doesn't mean we ought automatically to go along with the dog's view, rather that we need to consider it before coming to a conclusion and responding hastily to something we object to. Once we understand how the dog sees things, we can set limits on behavior, if needed. Above all, in the midst of feeling annoyed or frustrated, we need to recover our patience.

CHAPTER FIVE

AT WORK WITH DOGS

If you dream that a dog is searching you out,
you will be offered interesting work.

French proverb

I'm late for work, so I grab my gear, run out to the car, and do a last-minute inventory to make sure I haven't forgotten something. I've got my hat, coat, umbrella (looks cloudy!), briefcase, some books I need, Dog. *Dog?*

A dog at work?

Many dog lovers have realized that dogs are happiest when they have a purpose. Some dogs have jobs of their own—guarding sheep, pulling sleds, guiding a blind person. Others accompany us while we work. Their job is us.

Michele borrows her friend's dogs because she finds her New York studio apartment too confining to have her own. She puts it this way: "Dogs need a mission. Whether it's tearing up the couch or whatever, they need a mission." Michele's best friend Laura got a dog, christened Mandog by Michele, to provide a steadying presence in her chaotic household. Two kids, a commuting husband, her own twice-weekly commute to her office in New York City, and working at home the rest of the time kept her busy. What would the dog's mission be, Michele wondered? "It began with him hanging out on the floor while Laura worked at her computer. After a while he began to lay across her feet. After a few weeks that became Mandog's mission—keeping Laura focused while she worked. If she's up all hours working on a deadline, he sleeps on her feet." Laura told Michele, "As long as he's on my feet I know I'm supposed to be working. If he gets up and needs to go outside, I know it's time for me to get up and go for a walk outside and stretch my legs. When we come back in he settles down again." The natural inner rhythms of Laura's dog remind Laura to attend to her own.

The first dog Allan and Angie got cost seven dollars at the local humane society in Toronto. "People still talk about him in my business," Allan said. "I took him with me when I went on the road selling books—and used him shamelessly in my sales methods. I remember a librarian I called on in northern Ontario who liked dogs. If it was forty below or something, I'd mention casually that I had a dog in the car, and she'd tell me to bring him in. She loved to see him. She'd be buying books and she'd say, "I'll take one of that." "Well, wouldn't two be better?" I'd suggest. She'd look at Blue and answer, "Yes, two would be nice." Whenever she called me she'd ask, "How are you? How is your dog Blue?"

"When a dog comes along as part of a salesman's visit, it breaks the monotony of people's work routines. It becomes a part of their expectations of seeing you," Angie noted. Blue's presence added a distinctive character to Allan's business and made it stand out in people's minds.

Rob, no longer at the nursing home or studying biology, is now general manager of an electrical manufacturing plant. He agrees that a pet can change the pace of work for the better. The dog needs to be both "very comfortable with the surroundings and to think she owns the place. Katie lets us know when someone is coming. She knows the UPS and Federal Express drivers—they're okay with her, but she still gives her little alert-protection bark as if she's saying, 'Somebody's here, you'd better take care of them.'" Katie has her routine down pat. "There's one fellow she likes to eat lunch with, so in the morning she says hello to him to let him know she's arrived, something like, 'Don't forget I'm here when you go to lunch.' Then she waits for my dad; she has a certain bark for him when he comes in. When it's time for our walk, she puts her nose on my leg. After the walk she has another lunch with my dad, then lies down on her bed under my desk. About five minutes before the day ends, she comes and gets me to let me know it's time to leave."

Morgan uses Fantom to help make managing his company more personal. "When it's been a long, difficult day and I have to tell somebody who has just pulled off a stunt, 'We don't do that here,' I pull out a brush and brush the dog. It beats the heck out of walking back and forth to burn off a little irritation. So the person comes in and sees a really nice-looking dog. We discuss the problem and they say, 'That's a gorgeous dog … Hey, I'm sorry I irritated you.'" Morgan's dog provided an opportunity to let people see him in a new way.

Fantom provides a second benefit—he keeps people from boring Morgan. "Fantom has a low pain threshold. If there's a meeting going on and someone monopolizes the conversation by droning on and on, Fantom, who is usually under the table, will moan loudly. He will shut anyone up, because there is no way anyone can talk through it."

Chelsea accompanied Gard to his university office, particularly in summertime when she'd otherwise be home alone. Then the university rules were changed and Gard was faced with leaving the dog home. Initially, Gard was angry because he brought Chelsea to school less for his sake than for hers. "I've got plenty of stimulation in my life—people coming and going, reading, phones, everything else. But she doesn't. If it were me sitting at home all day, just staring out the window, I'd get really bored. I think dogs are no different from us—if they don't use their brain, it gets dull. The life goes out of them and they're not as lively." He still brings her with him to the lab and at night to his office. "Everybody here at night knows her. If they like dogs, that's cool. If they don't, they don't stop by to see me." Since Gard keeps Chelsea in his office, contact with her by others is voluntary. As long as co-workers and visitors don't feel coerced into an unwished-for involvement with our pets, they are likely at least to accept their presence and, perhaps, with time, come to seek them out.

Making work human

When you have your own business, your time is free—you can work any eighty hours a week you choose. Or at least that's the way it can sometimes feel when all the responsibility lies on your shoulders and you don't know where or when the next customer is coming from. The stress can build up to gut-wrenching levels. For a dog lover, one nice perk is that it's up to you whether you bring your dog to work or not.

Maggie, a working-girl Scottie, goes with Julie to her publishing business every day, thriving in a very stressful environment. "Some days work is overwhelming," Julie said, emphatically. "Publishing can be a risky business, but Maggie makes a big difference by relieving the pressure. My partner might be struggling with a contract, or we'll be searching for a solution to a thorny problem. Maggie will just wake up out of a dead sleep, walk over to Tamara's desk barking and demanding to play. So we play ball for a while—the dog gives us permission. It's as though she senses the tension in the air and feels compelled to relieve it. On the surface I think, 'What are we doing? We're wasting ten minutes playing ball!' But it has a rejuvenating effect. Somehow the stress melts away and we can sit back and say, okay, it's not that bad. Let's figure it out."

Running a messenger service and a hub telephone center for seven other messenger companies can be nerve-wracking. Describing his work environment, Michael began, "The nerve center is a small room with six operators working in it. It can get very tense. An operator may pick up the phone and have someone blasting away on the other side." As soon as he arrives with his Jack Russell Terrier, Jib, everyone relaxes totally. "They see him, pet him, and he makes them smile—it changes their whole day. People go out of their way to see Jib when they're on break. I didn't expect that to happen, and it's not the reason I brought him to work—I just wanted to be with him." After a while, a few other dogs began coming to work as well. "They have doggie playtime; they all go into a central room and wrestle around. It breaks up the day, keeps it from being work, work, work, allows playful moments to enter."

Fortunately, no one in his office is highly allergic or negatively disposed toward dogs. "Mostly, the dogs stay right at the desks of the people who bring them, unless they go where they can all play around." Michael personally finds it "very comforting to know my friend is there. If I get off the phone and the conversation hasn't gone well or was very challenging, well, he's right there. And helps me to work through creative problems."

Nancy Dusseau left her job at a law office to start a venture capital firm. "I took the dogs with me a couple of days a week, usually on rainy days when they would have been stuck in the house. One of my partners started bringing his two Dobermans once in a while. Most everyone in the office loved having them. "When they're around I don't take some things quite so seriously. It's hard to pat a dog's head and scream at someone while you're talking on the phone. How self-important can you be with your hand on a dog's head?"

Bonnie began commuting with her dog to make the long drive delightful and to keep from leaving him home alone. Then, between therapy clients, walking the dog helped relieve the intensity of her work. She found that Duke "immediately tuned in to how he should behave, who was important in the room, who he could go to for a pat on the head, and who wasn't up to it." She'd read about the healing effect dogs could have and now saw for herself how sensitive her dog was. That led her to consider bringing her other dog to a session with a family. "My client, the young man in the family, was very anxious about the session. I took Lucy with me because I knew she would break the tension. I let her be a little out of control for about five minutes until she demanded to be petted and jumped onto the young man's lap. It worked exactly the way I hoped it would. He had Lucy with him as an ally without seeming less mature, and he was able to be less anxious."

Lynn Vaughan, the licensed massage therapist, says her animals have been instrumental in helping people progress in their healing. Her dog Beau—nicknamed Beau-zo because he's so outgoing and deliberately goofy—butts in at just the right time. "I remember a woman who had been battered," Lynn said. "Because touch was potentially threatening, having bodywork was very difficult for her. Beau found his way into the massage room, jumped up on the table, and lay down on top of her. It started us laughing and she relaxed immediately." On another occasion, she was working with a man who had been physically disabled in a bad accident and had lost his speech. "Beau would lie on top of his chest, plastered to him, with his head in the man's face, licking him. The man would break into laughter. I could communicate with my client through his joy with the dog." Bonnie and Lynn might never have discovered their dogs' potential for healing if they hadn't brought them along to their workplaces. Fortuitously, the benefit they felt got passed along to their clients very directly.

Take a dog break

Computer screens can hypnotize and numb: having no experience of time they never tire and never need a rest. Each year, ever-faster processors further relieve the deadly waits for a large database to sort or a web page to load. But their speed also increases the amount of information our human brains must process. We get trapped in never-ending cycles of work done in the computer's timeless world.

One who tends to work nine or ten solid hours, Barbara never took a break, not even for lunch. "My longest break was going to grab a soda from the soda machine." Then she began bringing her dog to work. "Now I find that after two or three hours of work, she pokes at my shoulder to get some attention. We take a minimum of one break a day, usually two, to go outside and throw a tennis ball, or play with the other dogs. I've stopped for ten or fifteen minutes, gotten some sunlight and fresh air. Even if I only stop to pet her for a couple of minutes, it really reduces the stress. It's like someone tapping you on the shoulder, telling you that everything is going to be okay. I would think twice about ever working for a company where I couldn't bring my dog to work."

Lyssa can also spend all day long at the computer writing reports in her home office. If she does, "Sophie comes up to me and puts her head under my elbow. I tell her to quit, but then I'll look up and see that I've been writing for hours. Sophie wasn't telling me she needed a break, she was telling me that *I* needed one. Then I think, 'Good point! Good dog!'" Ttaka performs the same service for Melissa, who writes and edits with her dog at her side. "I get lost in what I'm doing. I forget that I need to stand up and stretch, that I need to eat and drink, or walk around. But every couple of hours, Ttaka tells me she needs to go outside by scratching and staring a hole through me. That gets me up and walking." In addition to the physical side of the exercise, Melissa has found that "if I let her walk me without a set route in mind, it serves as a kind of meditation—I don't have to be thinking. When she wants to go in a certain direction, I don't say no. If I discover that I have an agenda, I abandon it and let her lead where she wants and stop and sniff as many times as she wants. I let her do whatever it is she wants to do so she can be as fulfilled as possible, and I get to mind-break completely."

Corporate dogs

Even if you don't own your own business, you may get to bring your dog to work. Some corporations have adopted polices allowing employees to have pets accompany them. The basic question many people have about bringing dogs to work is: Will the dog steal your heart or your lunch?

Craig gives workshops on creativity in the corporate setting. One of his recommendations is that a company begin having "Pet Days." Initially, people are often puzzled and ask what they do on that day. "Just bring your pets to work," he tells them.

"But then what?" they ask.

"Work."

"And the dogs will do what?"

"They'll just be there," he explains. After a pause he turns to his dog, holds out a stack of papers, and continues, "Schatzi—fourteen copies, stapled and collated." At that point Craig says, "they usually begin to understand that the dogs offer opportunities not only to make a particular task more fun, but a chance to stop and laugh."

At AutoDesk, every day is Pet Day. The company was founded in 1982 by a group of programmers who found themselves working twelve- or fourteen-hour days. Some of them wanted to have their dogs with them so they wouldn't have to worry about being home to feed them or take them out. The practice has become a part of the company culture— a benefit for AutoDesk employees, on a par with benefits for people who have children, want to work at home, need eldercare, or use an on-site gym. At any given time there are probably around seventy-five dogs in an eight hundred-employee office. Joe, Catherine, and Yvette speak for many AutoDesk people.

Joe, a programmer at AutoDesk, told us that "in a kind of stereotypical way I sit at the computer all the time, eating lunch at my desk and working straight through. I brought my dog into work when she was still a puppy. That made for a big change—taking frequent potty breaks, feeding and training her. I had to get up and out, give her a little exercise, and really take a break myself." After bringing his dog to work for two and a half years, Joe finds it hard to remember what things were like without her. "Having her with me is a stress-reducer; she helps me take a step back from the day's activities, whether from politics or a poor decision someone has made. I'll see her face and just for a while, it makes me think of something other than work, and that there are other things of value."

Catherine befriended many dog people at AutoDesk and takes breaks with them and their dogs. Additionally, she said, "I've always felt that it's much easier to go up to a manager or VP when they are with their dog and make dog talk as a nice way to get acquainted. I just really enjoy it. Now I just can't quit my job—they've got me by the neck!"

Yvette has heard AutoDesk people say the dogs bring some feeling into work, a bit of real life, a reality check. "Even on the worst days, when I'm totally frustrated and on the verge of tears, I have to take my dog outside and sit down for a few minutes. Back inside, none of the 'stuff' seems as important. What would be just another job at a computer in a big building becomes more human—or is it more canine? " Most of the non-dog people feel positively about the dogs. They get to see them and go home without any concerns about food or cleaning up after them—all of the benefits and none of the responsibilities. "Sometimes someone comes to my cube while I'm working to sit and visit with Kasey. Once I realize that they're down on their knees—talking to her—by choice, I just go on working." Companies are adopting "bring your pet" policies but they aren't numerous yet. "People e-mail us asking for our rules because they want to start a program at their place of work. We send a copy, but I don't know whether or not they implement them."

Lisa recently left her job at AutoDesk for a job at a company that doesn't allow dogs. She has been concerned about the difficulties both she and her dog Blarney will have. "I've had a very special situation for the last five years working with Blarney, so it's tough making the transition. People say, 'Oh your dog can sit at home for three days.' That's not the point! I want to feel that he's having the fullest life and that he's having fun. I'm concerned that this may cause him to get older quicker. I'm sure that going to work with me kept him young mentally." When Lisa's husband Nick telecommutes from his home office two days a week, he'll be with Blarney and make things easier for him.

Overcoming problems

Some people either don't like dogs or think dogs don't like them, so they prefer not to be around them. They may complain about off-leash dogs or messes in the halls. Exercising common sense and courtesy, we can defuse most incidents and help others accept the presence of our dogs without feeling we're inflicting them on them.

At AutoDesk, so many employees brought their pets that some rules were needed to make things easier for everyone. Joe ticked off a few of these. "You can't have a dog with fleas. You can't have a mean dog. If a dog makes a mess or two, the owner has to get some training and show that the problem has been solved. For the most part the rules are followed, but people still let their dogs off leash. No one wants to be the bad guy and say, 'Get that dog on a leash.'" Joe thought a few other rules were also helpful. "If you're not in your office, your dog must be either shut in or tied up in your cube; you take your dog outside to go to the bathroom; you pick up after your dog (the receptionists even have doggy bags at their desks for this purpose); and dogs aren't allowed in meetings, the cafeteria, or dining areas."

Morgan has a way of turning some difficulties around creatively. "Around ten thirty A.M. every day, I let Fantom out of harness to run back and forth in the hall to burn off energy. I simply yell, 'Dog in the hall!' and let him run. Often, someone on my team goes down to the other end of the hall, grabs him by the collar, and tells him to 'Run!' pulling on the collar as if throwing a bowling ball. We call it 'bowling puppies.' It's probably disrespectful, because he runs like a bat to the other end of the hall—on really slick polished tile. You'll hear him turn to the side and slam in to the wall. But he likes it! Frequently he thinks it would be fun to run into you, so he'll try to put on the brakes and turn sideways just before he gets to you. If you don't turn out of his way, you will have a football injury you will never forget.

"It's a ton of pleasure and it makes people feel good—as long as you're careful not to startle someone," Morgan points out, exhibiting a sense of responsibility that complements his sense of humor.

In all the work situations we've looked at, the spontaneity of the dogs, their disinterested presence, and above all the recognition by others that the person bringing the dog has chosen to allow an affectionate relationship to enter the work environment, has changed the quality of the workplace. The affection between human and dog does not have the potential for being as disruptive to work as does an intimate relationship between two humans. As we complete the transition to a service-based economy, the caring embodied in the human-dog relationship taken into the workplace can add an invaluable sensitivity to the rendering of service. Dogs at work can be a "win-win" event.

CHAPTER SIX

PARTNERS IN WORK

When the dog is awake, the shepherd may sleep.

German proverb

Dogs not only accompany us to work for company, but also they work with and for us. Perhaps, as bonds formed between us in prehistory, their first job was rousing us from sleep when danger approached. As their companionship endured over the course of many thousands of years, we came to recognize their driving passions and harnessed those passions to our own. Dogs watch and guard, they herd and protect, they lead the way and counsel, they chase and hunt.

The bonds that form between people and working dogs are among the oldest and deepest. The work we can do with dogs is "old" work, pre-technical work with clear beginnings, middles, and ends: rich in sensitivity to the pleasures of purposeful physicality; satisfying in the profound unity of purpose between dogs and us; unburdened by the conflicting motives we must accommodate when we work with other people. So deep is the connection that often words do not come easily to express it, that is why some people who work with dogs may be seen as unfeeling or callous. Those who speak here can attest to an eloquent bond between dogs who love their work and their people, and the people who work with and love them.

Ranching and herding

Driving in the Southwest on Indian lands, a traveler can still come upon a flock of twenty or thirty sheep attended by an elderly woman who seems hardly able to keep up with or care for them. A second look reveals a dog constantly on the move, reining in strays, shaping the flock, almost gliding on legs that never pause or tire, connected to the woman by ties so fine they are invisible to the uninitiated. Bonnie, who grew up on a Northern California ranch watching her stepfather Hap work with his dogs and horses, came to understand that connection.

"The communication between them was unbelievable," she remembered. "The dogs would lead the horses, taking precedence over them. It was 'man-dog-horse.' The cattle dogs, McNabs, he called them, were just lovely. They were like a big Labrador with big heads, often black with short hair. With just a tip of the hat or a nod from Hap, they'd be off circling five hundred head of cattle. If the horses didn't co-operate, the dogs would nip the backs of their legs. Using minute indications among themselves, these three—man, dog, and horse—would manage a huge herd."

The reciprocity between her stepfather Hap and his dog Shorty extended to dessert. "One evening mom made some ice cream and handed Hap a dish. Hap took a bite. Shorty took a bite. Each portion was taken in halves. Shorty only took his half of what was left, and Hap only took his own half. The half portions just kept getting smaller. When it got down near the bottom, Hap held the bowl for Shorty to lick up his share. Shorty understood the reciprocal nature of what they were doing."

The depth of the connection between Hap and his dogs was illuminated for Bonnie when one of his dogs was hit by a car. "It's the only time I've ever seen Hap rude around a woman," Bonnie said. "She'd been careless and wasn't apologetic enough. I remember Hap, this giant cowboy, carrying the limp animal, tears streaming down his face. He was a man who rarely ever cried or showed emotion. To give an indication of his character, about ten years ago he died of a brain tumor, but because he didn't want to linger, he refused to eat until he died. He was a cowboy of the original breed. . . ."

Michael also experienced ranch life, spending summer and spring vacations on his grandfather's ranch near Telluride in Colorado, a place very different from the Sacramento suburb where he lived. "He took care of the perimeter of large areas of empty rangeland. Grandfather made sure the fences were up, the salt licks were out, and that no cattle or sheep had died or been injured. There were Basque herders in the area, and he made sure they were all right, bringing supplies in from town for them. Dogs were half-working partner and half-companion for him. They helped break the monotony of working alone in large stretches of land where it was just him and the sheep or cattle.

"The kinds of things I'd see them doing were work-related. The dogs knew when to get out, when to stay in the car, when it was time to play. They knew when it was a serious time, too, and they worked together really well. They knew which people were friendly and which weren't. Grandfather had a lot of faith and unspoken interaction with the dogs that other people just didn't understand. There were a lot of gestures; only occasionally would he use words.

"They knew his truck by the look and sound. When he drove into town, they would come running. He didn't have to call them, he'd just drive down main street and the two dogs would jump into the truck while it was still moving. His two dogs sat in the passenger seat, so if I wanted to be part of the group, I really had to squeeze to get into the cab."

The duo of human and working dog is often so tight—so much time is spent together that an intimate and responsive understanding develops—that the dogs are often treated by their partners as the equals of other humans. Michael's and Bonnie's good-natured acceptance of this reality let them come to understand the bonds formed between the working partners.

Hunting

On every part of the earth's surface where there are people and dogs, dogs hunt with us. It is the oldest and most continuous working partnership between our species. As a surveyor, Paul Webb spends much of his time outdoors, often with his Labrador, Ben, and he likes to hunt when he has the time. He strongly believes that dogs need a purpose. "A dog that lives all its life without purpose other than to gratify his appetite and his master's desire for a pet won't be a happy dog. He's like an unemployed person with low self-esteem. So give him both—have him as a pet *and* give him a purpose, a job."

There are two schools of thought about how to keep hunting dogs. One says, don't get too close to your dog because you want to discipline him whenever he needs it: keep the dog outside in a kennel to acclimate it to cold weather and to develop its stamina. The other says, develop the bond so that the dog wants to work for you: keep the dog inside the house and take him with you wherever you go. Hal, a photographer, belongs to the second school. "My dogs have the run of the house and I can tell you that Quinn, my old guy, was every bit as good a hunter as any dog I've ever seen. He could stay out in the cold, in rain and snow all day without showing any signs of being cold or fatigued."

Any dog bred for it loves hunting with a passion. At one time, Hal's other dog, Reilly, was injured so he couldn't hunt, and Hal had to sneak out. "If Reilly thought I went hunting without him it would break his heart. Reilly and Quinn are delighted to be on this earth and especially to be able to go hunting."

Hunting dogs can tune their work so finely to their masters' wishes that an unspoken gratitude and affection arises instantaneously. We heard in Hal's voice as he told of their exploits the deep attachment and love he feels for his dogs. "I respect their big hearts," he began. "I was hunting, it was snowing, and at the very end of the day we needed two more ducks to reach our limit. I shot one and it fell into the worst cover imaginable—dense tulles, cattail-like reeds growing in water. Quinn just disappeared for forty-five minutes. Finally, about two minutes before closing time, he came out like a submarine from under the water, with tulles, weeds, roots, and everything draped all over his head—with the duck in his mouth." But Quinn's effort wasn't over yet. "Suddenly, he stopped, sat down still, never letting go of the duck and pointed up, alerting me to another duck flying over my head, which I got. Movement scares the birds, so he knew he had to be motionless. He's done things like that hundreds of times."

Police work

While dangerous situations may arise from time to time in many dog occupations, danger is the stuff of the job itself for police dogs. The relationship between dog and handler is intensified by the situation of putting the dog in jeopardy. Pat, the dog handler in the Oakland Police Department, thinks it's the best job an officer can have. He put the uniqueness of the relationship this way: "You have this dog who is willing to give his life for you without thinking and, on virtually every call, you put the dog, as well as yourself, in harm's way. Of course, we work as safely as we can. I don't want anybody to get shot. But the possibility always exists.

"The dog is not doing it for any civic good or any of the things that a police officer does it for—to catch criminals so nobody else gets hurt, and so forth. The dog only does it out of love and loyalty for the handler. We go and we do a good job. We catch a criminal and I tell him 'Good boy' and pat him on the head. That's good enough for him. The better we are as a team, the more that cuts down the chances of anybody getting hurt."

According to Pat, loyalty is a two-way street. "I know from past experience that unless Gitan was locked up in a kennel or in the car, he would never let any harm come to me if there was any way he could intervene. It's same for me—I would never let anything happen to him. I remember searching some old buildings in west Oakland where the escalator stairs had been ripped out, exposing the gears and machinery for three stories. He rounded a corner, slipped, and started to fall into the machinery. I reached out and grabbed him by the collar, balancing on the edge for a second until I could pull him back up. Later, thinking about it, I wondered if someone else would have just said, 'I'd better wait or let him fall, that's too bad.' There have been times when he found the suspect we were looking for and he got beaten—once with a metal folding chair and once with a board. Some of those men had guns or knives. The thought never crossed my mind, 'This is too dangerous, I better just leave and hope he makes his way out of it.'"

People usually don't think of police dogs as sleeping on the bedroom floor next to their masters, as well as going to work at night and biting somebody on command. "What police departments and police dog handlers actually look for is not a big wild, vicious, frightening Tasmanian devil of an animal but a dog that will go out, do the job to the best of his abilities, and then be a regular dog when he's not working. My dog for instance is actually a big baby. We do presentations in grade schools for kindergarten classes on up where the kids get to pet him, walk him around, and pull on his ears and tail. When he's at home he usually plops in a corner by the TV. My wife takes him when she goes for walks; he goes along, a happy dog. But if I pick up the keys he's up instantly: 'Oh, are we going to work today?'"

Pat beams, "You get to work with him. You get to have him at home. You get to play with him. So you get everything, the best of all worlds."

Therapy dogs

Therapy dogs enter into less dangerous but no less intense situations. Beezus, a Golden Retriever belonging to the niece of Deborah Jones, had a calling in life. Deborah thought he'd make a great therapy dog, a hunch confirmed by his obedience trainer. "So we volunteered," Deborah said, "and went to the hospital to do a group therapy session. One woman was agitatedly talking—trying to express herself about something we couldn't understand. Beezus went to her, jumped up, laid across her chest, and licked her face, giving her some good loving. Exactly what she needed. She calmed down and he walked away."

At two years old, Beezus has grown expert at assessing a situation and responding to it. "Now he is over at UCLA hospitals and we got assigned to two intensive care units. He drags me down the hall to get there. He wants to play with the staff and jump around and get rubbed. Then when it's time for patient visits, he crawls up into their beds and snuggles up, licks their hand a couple of times, lays his head across their belly, and lets them rub him. Another patient was unable to speak and could only move the big toe on his right foot. When Beezus gently climbed onto his bed, the man raised his right hand to pet Beezus, bringing cries of excitement from the patient's wife, and a beaming grin and tear-filled eyes from the patient himself."

Guide dogs

One of the oldest professions for assistance dogs is that of guiding blind people. Stacey has been training guide dogs for many years, and now supervises other trainers. "Working with animals is very humbling. It's not like working with something static. Guide dogs are so willing, although you do come across obstinate dogs. Yet with experience you realize that obstinacy is actually confusion indicating that you aren't teaching the dog appropriately. You should always turn it around and look at what you're not doing correctly or not making clear."

Stacey is sensitive to the unique differences among the many dogs she has trained or supervised the training of. "Some dogs you connect with more. Other dogs you just don't much like—you think. They're all individuals in terms of energy levels, personality, responsiveness, sensitivity. There are some dogs I may consider just a little 'silly' or immature; they're dogs I end up working with more. Once the dog demonstrates a willingness and animation, working with it actually ends up being a pleasure. You end up loving all your dogs and appreciating them for what they have—and don't have. You can find a redeeming quality in every dog."

Despite all of Fantom's idiosyncrasies and playfulness, he's a working dog. He and Morgan have been working together for a year and a half, yet Morgan feels that "the thrill of just being in his company is very fresh. People can get used to each other, and then ... it's not that they fall out of love, but it changes a little. You get used to working with them and they become more of a partner. With Fantom, there is still that part, but he'll hop up and put his paws on my shoulders and I'll just hug him, a big body hug. Guide dogs aren't supposed to hop up, of course, but I don't discourage it. It's great, and it's one of the things we'll do every morning at about ten thirty. It's just the neatest thrill."

"When he's in harness and I tell him 'forward,' from that point we're working and he is my eyes," Morgan explained.

"A good guide dog takes pride in its work. They know they're working! I don't know if the dog knows I'm blind, but he certainly knows he has to lead me around and that if he runs me into a tree I'm going to pop his leash a bit, tell him 'no,' shake the limb, and we'll re-work it so he remembers to look up. It's hard for a dog to remember to look up, but he's supposed to do that. I go all over the place, I travel all over the country, and I expect Fantom to work very hard because I do. Fantom enjoys working. He *runs* into his harness—usually. He likes to run at it and swerve out of the way, and I have to tell him we don't do things that way.

"He just shines—you can just feel him snap to attention when I say 'Forward, Fantom.' He has that attitude of 'I'm ready, I'm ready—let's go kick some butt. What do you want me to do? Just give me the orders.' I play the superior role when we work because I'm alpha dog, but that doesn't make us any less close. That's the difference between leadership and domination. So many people feel they have to dominate their dogs. I think that's a shame."

Morgan and Stacey have recognized that dominating a dog fosters dependence and subservience—and possibly an opposing rebellion born of frustration—rather than the spirit of cooperation needed to respond flexibly in novel situations.

Teaming with sled dogs

Teams of Canadian Inuit dogs, the original sled dogs, were responsible for the Eskimos becoming the world's only circumpolar culture. Teams of Malamutes, Siberian Huskies, Samoyeds, and mixed breeds joined them as draft dogs who made living in the far north possible.

In 1991, an international treaty governing Antarctica contained a clause mandating the removal of all non-native species, except for humans. There was a slim possibility that the dogs might transmit canine distemper to seals. "It was the end of an era," John told us. He first fell in love with dogs working as an electrician at Moffin Station in Antarctica and was there when the sled dogs were removed. "The time they left was highly emotional. There were a lot of sad faces around, people crying. They were so attached to the dogs. We didn't go outdoors as much because there wasn't any excitement. I hate to run, but give me a dog team and I'll run beside them all day. When we did go outside we had to take some sort of vehicle—noisy and fast, and we were enclosed in a crash hel-met or sat behind a fogged up windscreen. Is it snowing or windy? You wouldn't know. With the dogs gone, everyone was a bit vacant, more insulated—watching videos, reading books, and playing on computers. It was a real shame. They were no longer experiencing the beauty and challenge of trav-eling and camping out there in the elements. With a dog team you experience all these things, islands and icebergs always coming into view and going past."

Some of those dogs went to Paul Scherke. "The Austra-lian research teams had to find homes for their dogs, so they sent a couple of their station administrators on a tour of the far north to look for candidate homes. One was ours, here at Wintergreen Lodge in Ely, Minnesota. They said they liked what we did and we agreed to accept some of the Antarctic team, while another dog sledding operation in Minnesota agreed to take the others. The older dogs found homes in Australia."

Paul spoke of his long experience with sled dogs on expeditions to both Poles, and of eighteen years arranging adventure travel trips through the woods. "With these dogs, you work together seriously. Mushing [driving] a sled isn't a passive activity for the person on board. You're pulling on the back of the sled, leveraging with your feet and your arms to steer and assist it over obstacles, and working with the dogs to get it around corners and up steep hills. The dogs are very much aware that the effort engaged in pulling the sled involves their human companions and all the animals in the team working in concert. When you accomplish your task together, it's not just sharing enjoyment, it's sharing a goal and succeeding in a mission."

People develop one type of relationship with their playmates, another with their workmates. Each relationship may be deep, yet each has different qualities, and we experience them differently. Paul reflected on the differences between his pet dogs and his sled dogs. "Sled dogs really love to run. They like to be out seeing new things, puffing and panting away. They'll work for you as hard as they can for as long as they can, in all conditions, from warm to cold to windy. There are so many differences between a pet dog and a working dog that they could be a different species altogether, and our connection with them is different as well. My family and I share a relationship with our Golden Retriever, similar to one most people share with their pets. We enjoy playing together—throwing sticks or balls or running around the woods. But the dogs in our kennel are truly draft animals. They have the same affinity, intensity of affection, and connection with us that our Golden Retriever has, but their instinct to work, to be in harness and pull, is the most compelling aspect of their nature. Given a choice between getting some affection or having a chance to pull the sled, they'll take the sled. When the first snow falls, it's the fun event of the year because on that day, for the first time in months, we hear them erupt in a group howl with a cheery tone to it."

Julie discovered the truth of Paul's assertion when she went on a three-day dog sled expedition with a group of people from different parts of the U.S. and Canada. Her biggest shock was accepting the dogs as working dogs. "I wanted to do the trip because I loved dogs so much. When we arrived, I was taken aback—the dogs were in kennels, outside, in the cold! But when the dogs were being selected, I realized they were totally different from dogs I had known. The moment they saw the sleds and the people they knew what was going on—somebody was going for a run. The dogs just went nuts, they so clearly loved to run. Then I started feeling sorry for the dogs who didn't get to go."

First the novices made dry runs and learned a little about handling the dogs and sleds. "One by one, they led us onto the trail. The dogs whooshed out with us hanging on—it was like being shot out of a cannon! We sailed through the woods. All I could hear was the sled against the snow and the dogs panting. As I got to know them better, they were more responsive and would pull for me. They ran and ran and ran, without getting tired. It was amazing. When they pulled us up hills, I got off the sled and ran alongside because I was afraid the dogs had too much weight to pull up the hill—but they were happy as clams."

Julie got to know the idiosyncrasies of a dog team. As Paul described it, "The dogs aren't like cars; you can't just turn on the engine and off you go. They have personalities and traits, good and bad days. Like most things in life, the goal is not getting where you're going, it's what happens along the way. If dogs were just pulling machines, it would be pointless to undertake the additional hassles and headaches of maintaining a team of dogs to go a few miles through the woods. You could keep a snowmachine in the garage all summer and just throw in some gas in the winter and go."

"It's all part of the science, beauty and the art of running dogs," John summed up. In September 1997 he'll begin the International Greenland Expedition, a nine-month trek with his partner and their dogs, sledding and skiing alongside the dogs. "You work for them as well as they work for you. You become part of a team, a nucleus heading toward one goal—

to try to get to where you want to go and do what you have to do. The dogs like you to run along behind them, talking to them, telling them 'Good dog!' Guiding them by calls, you tell them, 'Go right!" and they look over their shoulder to see if they're doing the right thing. "Good dog," you tell them, again. They don't actually speak to you, but if you can just get that vibe ... it's great."

"Dogs help people stay alive. Machines break down; I've never had to call for help when I was running a dog team. Dogs can detect areas of bad ice, or where there are big crevasses, or where the ice is thin. You might break through with a machine. Traveling along the coast of Antarctica, they remember very well where the food caches are even though they might not have been there for a year or more. You'll be looking at your map to navigate and they're veering off. You try to pull them back, but they persist in their direction. Before you know it, you're at the food cache, and it's not where you thought it would be!"

The intense partnership that develops between sled dogs and people, while of the same nature as those formed in other working relationships, are particularly close because the rigors of the Arctic or Antarctic constantly challenge the very existence of warm-blooded creatures such as ourselves.

Where machines have replaced dogs, the environment has grown ever so much colder.

CHAPTER SEVEN

LESSONS IN LIVING

The dog is a true philosopher.

Socrates

We learn something from our dogs with nearly every wag of their tails. Most lessons are small ones, small gains in sensitivity that make our everyday experience a little richer, a little more colorful. A few lessons leave a powerful imprint on how we see things and affect what we do. Either type of lesson may occur as a sudden, unbidden insight, or may develop gradually until a moment arrives when we realize that our point of view has shifted, that we've learned something. Perhaps we recognize a connection between what we feel about the dog or how we're treating it and some aspect of ourselves that we hadn't previously acknowledged, such as closed-mindedness or irresponsibility.

Simplicity

Complication abounds in all our lives—from the arcane rules of filling in an income tax form to programming a VCR to tape a show we want to see. *Complication* differs from *complexity*. Complication always reveals itself as shallow and empty; complexity is rich and deep and, ultimately, has at its core, simplicity. The simplicity of dogs is a constant reminder of our complications, as well as our complexity, and serves as a call to attend to the heart of matters. "Dogs," Joe said, "have very few needs and wants. I'm just the opposite—materialistic, petty, and other terrible things—but having my dog around helps me gain a bit of perspective. I get reminded of simple pleasures." Sheila, an acupuncturist and body-worker, spoke of the simplest pleasure of all. "Dogs can get us back in the present moment. We start noticing the dimensions of where we are right now so we can become responsible for everything we give out or take in."

We need to begin by reciprocating what dogs offer. "If you reared kids and just gave them food and shelter and taught them proper education, you'd probably end up with a likable person," Patrice maintained. "But if you listened to that child, you could learn from him or her. You'd have to take the time to watch and listen. When a dog looks at you, they're *looking* at you and really want to know you." We often find openness easier to experience and enact toward dogs than toward people. "I feel so happy, enthusiastic, and open with dogs," Lynn reflected. "I could greet people the same way, but I expect many of them would be suspicious—interpersonal relationships are so much more complicated! The openness of dogs always reminds me to try a little more with people."

How people interact with dogs can be a litmus test of their decency. Craig had inherited his two dogs with the purchase of his house, which needed a few repairs. "When contractors came to bid on work I'd watch how they paid attention to the dogs. I wouldn't hire contractors who didn't get along with them. From the previous owners, I'd inherited some workers who didn't treat the dogs well, so I hired new workers and first thing after arriving, they'd look for the dogs and spend five minutes being affectionate to them. I found that people who weren't civil to the dogs often didn't do well with human beings, either."

Uncomplicated and direct, a dog's feelings about people are easy to understand. Janet notes, "It's usually not hard to tell when a dog likes someone and when they don't. I've never seen a hypocritical dog—acting one way toward you and then 'talking behind your back' because they actually feel something else."

Living simply is an expression of a unity, or as Adam called it, "wholeheartedness." Adam's dog Patch "is wholehearted and never hypocritical, very easy-going, amiable. He wants to please. So, when he doesn't obey, the issue has almost always boiled down to my communicating in a way that he can't understand." A clinical psychologist, Adam has been interested in garnering impressions of how Patch responded to commands in different situations, and has learned how the communication of an unwitting contradiction complicated the situation. "From different ways he responded to me, I've learned what it means to mean what I say. I'd been puzzled because he didn't come sometimes when I called or sit when

I told him to sit. Gradually, I realized that I had given him a command that on some level I didn't expect him to obey. It's like calling my kids to dinner when I really expect them to dawdle. In the back of my mind I expect to get irritated with them and have to call them three times. I've heard that tone in my voice when dealing with others, and I've found that people learn to recognize whether I really mean what I'm saying or not.

"Patch is a great mirror, that shows me how I am when I approach him. It became clear that if I really intended for him to come—and expected it—he'd come. If I didn't, he came when he felt like it or he'd wait until I meant it."

Adam's insight can be a model for all of us. He didn't jump to the conclusion that Patch was being willfully disobedient or was distracted by a competing interest, nor did Adam justify the irritation he felt. If we quietly take in how our dogs respond to us, without explaining away their responses or trying to justify our own, dogs can reflect exactly the knowledge we need to know ourselves better.

Acceptance

Acceptance, tempered by patience, can transform our experience from that of merely enduring an event into one which strengthens us. "I've always been low on patience," Catherine admitted about training her dog, Kaya. "I've had to learn to let her learn whatever we're training her to do; I can't expect her to not pee in the house immediately. I have to be patient with her personality—she wants to play twenty-four hours a day! She'll jump on me, push me, poke me, or scratch at me, wanting attention. I'll tell her 'No,' and make her sit down. She'll stop for five minutes and then come back. She doesn't give up. I have to repeat myself, over and over again." Without her acceptance of Kaya's idiosyncrasies, Catherine would likely become a frustrated scold.

While Nathan's mother was working and putting herself through school in Chicago, Nathan, then six, and his twelve-year-old brother set up their own dog-sitting service. "My brother heard about a friend of a friend who had a business called Pet Vacations. Instead of bringing their dogs to kennels, they brought them to people's homes. My brother thought he could do it, too." The young dog-sitters lived in a little three-bedroom apartment. Their aunt had given them her dog, a Pekinese, very dominant and very majestic. "So we had this itty-bitty Pekinese and our regular dog-sitting clients—a Rhodesian Ridgeback, black Labs, German Shepherds—all full-bred show dogs. It was a lot of fun."

The family was just coming off welfare, so they had food stamps and dry milk. "One guy had us cook beefsteak for his dog. My brother and I looked at those beefsteaks and knew we couldn't have any. I loved all the dogs and they became extended family members . . . but they ate so much better than we did! I made a connection with them while feeding them these really extravagant meals, stirring wheat germ and cod liver oil in their food. The thing that was hard was I'd become attached to these dogs. With all pets they become family members, so these became extended family members." Incredibly, while others might have expressed their bitterness about the hardships of being poor and the inequities of caring for and pampering other people's dogs, Nathan spoke only of loving. "I was never bitten by a dog or felt threatened. If a dog growled or barked at me, I was respectful. They're like people: they have their turf—go there unannounced and they'll defend it. Very few dogs will attack you for no reason. If you treat a dog with a lot of respect, then you're bound to have a dog that respects you. We took good care of all the dogs, fed them, played with them, and loved them. All that came back."

Karen's dog, Comet, had every reason to feel bitter towards humans and reject them, since she'd been abandoned twice. "Yet she doesn't hold a grudge toward people. Instead, Comet is totally devoted and unreserved—she's not judgmental and is very positive about everything. I remember that on one of our first walks it was raining lightly but she walked with the same enthusiasm she had when it was sunny. To her, there was no difference between a rainy and a sunny day—she liked being outside and walking around. That was a lesson for me." Karen acknowledged her dog's acceptance, and rather than taking it for granted, she learned from it.

Caring for another

Caring for another being begins with the act of paying attention to it, becoming sensitive to it's needs. Paying attention to her dog while under stress was something Nancy Han made an effort to learn. She remembered an incident when she was showing her Kerry in the Beverly Hills dog show—a fancy show where she had to dress up. "I was a little nervous, not really listening to him, grooming him while he was wiggling around. He was trying to do something. The next thing I knew diarrhea shot right onto me, past me, everywhere. I screamed until friends came to my aid." They did their best to clean the dog with little concession napkins—not a pleasant endeavor. "People who don't pay attention to their dogs are probably like I was. I had my own stuff going on and didn't pay attention when my dog had to go to the bathroom. All relationships can be like that, but it's magnified in the dog-person relationship. People get what they need from the dog, but they don't notice what the dog needs from them."

As a "parent-in-training," Barbara learned what it's like to always be thinking about another creature, human or animal. "My husband and I are thinking about having kids in the next couple of years, and in some ways having a dog is a way to get ready. It helps us work through situations we don't agree on: discipline, housebreaking; whether to feed her table scraps. Originally, I said we shouldn't feed her scraps from the table because I didn't want her to beg. But she'd sit there and look at me and I'd give her treats. I tend to be lax on discipline; my husband is definitely more stringent." Barbara has given some thought to what will happen when the children arrive. "She's jealous toward me, more so than with my husband. If I play with another dog, she gets between us. And if I sit close to my husband? Although she's learned she has to sit *next* to us, she still tries to get *between* us. I know that kind of thing will happen when we have children. There will need to be a period of adjustment as she becomes used to another person in the house who gets attention. I'll continue taking her to work with me after we have kids, so she won't lose all her time with me. At home, however, she's going to have to share me."

Experienced at caring for her three children, Deborah Jacobs learned to better care for herself as well while acting as nurse to Lady. "After having some surgery, Lady had to wear one of those big plastic collars to prevent her tearing out stitches on her flank. A week into the healing process, we had a routine established. With the collar on, poor Lady couldn't lick her paws. So I was indulgent and took her collar off so she could eat or nose around outside, or lie down on her bed to lick her paws. Then I'd put the collar back on. I watched to make sure she wasn't at her stitches. But, once, I got distracted for a moment and by the time I turned back to her she'd ripped out some stitches. Unhappily, it was very difficult for her to be anesthetized for a second time in a week. I really hadn't done her any favor by indulging her." Deborah's realization didn't stop there. "I recognize the same feeling,

'Oh, poor me,' in myself as well. Through caring for my dog I learned something about myself: that being self-indulgent may undo weeks of effort. It isn't worth it."

Cooperation

G. I. Gurdjieff, a modern avatar who early in this century brought an ancient teaching to the West, twice had dogs as companions, each of whom he named Philos, the Greek word for friend. The first Philos was a large Kurd sheepdog who traveled with Gurdjieff throughout the East when he was a young man. The dog became famous in towns where Gurdjieff traveled for fetching him hot water in a kettle from taverns and going to shops bearing a note listing the supplies he wished to purchase. The second was a black and white mixed-breed who lived with Gurdjieff during the 1920s and 30s at the Prieuré, his château-ashram at Fontainebleau, just south of Paris. For a time Gurdjieff had a young boy, Fritz, as his special assistant.

Fritz became Philos's chosen companion during Gurdjieff's absences. When on gate duty, the children at the Prieuré enjoyed competing to see which of them, at Gurdjieff's return, would be alert enough to have the gates open so Gurdjieff could drive through without stopping. Eventually, Gurdjieff became aware of the game and began coasting down the hill noiselessly so the children would need to pay even more attention if they were to hear his approach.

Fritz noticed that while Philos merely pricked up his ears

at the sound of cars passing, he jumped to his feet when Gurdjieff's car approached, and so the boy was successful at opening the gate in time for the avatar's entrance. Gurdjieff, amused, asked Fritz how he was able to do it, and the boy told him about Philos. Gurdjieff replied that this was a good example of cooperation, a proof that people depend on other creatures, and have much to learn from dogs.

Trust

Acceptance, caring, cooperation: in time these qualities foster a relationship characterized by trust. Chelsea, the dog Gard rescued, had been not only abandoned, but also severely abused. "Chelsea taught me about trust, total and complete trust," Gard said. Torn up from the end of his marriage, Gard empathized instantly with Chelsea. Within their first hour of meeting, after Gard got down on all fours to play with her, Chelsea overcame her fears of him. "She probably sensed that I was hurting too, that I needed her as well. I approached her without any reserve. When you lie down on the ground and the dog is all over you with its mouth on your neck, you're totally vulnerable. She was gnawing on my head and ears and I was laughing." That experience was the first step in the bond of trust that formed between human and dog. "When I first rescued her and brought her home, she had to depend on me. I was all she had. And because I've never put her in a situation that would be damaging to her, she trusts what I tell her to do. If I told her to run out in the street when a car was coming, she'd do it. You don't find such complete trust too often in humans. Even in my own dealings with people there are certain hesitancies—I'm not willing to trust completely, whereas I will completely trust my dog."

Usually, dog people are receptive to meeting people: having them come up, pet their dog, and start a conversation. Some of us don't start out that way. Now on her way to becoming a veterinarian, Natasa said, "You have to break out of your shell, be receptive and friendly instead of snobbish. I was very shy when I was younger; it wasn't until I had a dog of my own, with most of the responsibility for walks, weekends to the beach, and regular vet visits, that I became more receptive. Now I love meeting people; even my friends have noticed."

A real estate agent by profession, Nancy Duff doesn't have a not-in-my-backyard outlook on life. She trusted her dog Yoda's judgment of a stranger, a trust that led her to see one man in a new way. "One winter I met this homeless guy," Nancy remembered, "a nice-looking young man who was living across the street in a parking lot. I'd walk by with my dog and eventually he began talking to me about Yoda. He asked if he could play ball with him and I said 'Okay.' Then he asked to take Yoda for a walk. I don't know why I said 'Okay' again." Nancy saw that Yoda liked the man and that the man clearly liked Yoda. At the time, she was living in one of two houses she'd remodeled and the front house was vacant. Based on Yoda's trust, Nancy came to a surprising decision. "It was cold and raining, and this kid is right across the street, in a sleeping bag, out in the open. I had an empty house—no furniture in it—what harm could he do? I said to him, 'You can sleep in here, in the front house.' When he told me he couldn't pay me anything, I told him he could take Yoda for walks a couple of times a day. He moved in and immediately got sick. Really sick. He'd barely been holding himself together. All he needed to get himself back together was a few months out of the cold without any pressure on him. Having a place out of the cold and having Yoda to hang out with—getting all that unconditional love from Yoda, meant a lot to him. So he slept on the floor for about three months, and when he felt better he got himself a job, then a place to live. Now he's married. This all took about a year ... and it was all through Yoda."

These dogs can be exemplars of qualities we wish for ourselves: simplicity, acceptance, caring, cooperation, trust. In the watchdog, endowed with the contradictory qualities of gentleness and spirit, Socrates found the requirements for the would-be guardians of his ideal state. Dogs welcome acquaintances yet bark at strangers, thereby distinguishing between friend and enemy, applying their test of knowledge and ignorance—which is what anyone who loves learning does. Equating love of learning with love of wisdom, Socrates pronounced dogs philosophers. No wonder we learn so much from our contact with them.

CHAPTER EIGHT

TO THE RESCUE

I am myself and what is around me,
and if I do not save it, it shall not save me.

José Ortega y Gasset

Passing by a stray at the side of the road can seem rational. Reason prompts, it's getting late, drive on, don't get involved—after all, animals can fend for themselves. The fact is they can't. We've domesticated dogs, selecting for skills at getting along within a human group, so they are no longer well-adapted to the wild. Consequently, we are responsible for their welfare, and if we abdicate that responsibility we lessen our humanity.

Routinely, dogs protect us and—thankfully not so often—save us from harm. In turn, many of us go out of our way to care for them, to rescue them when they are in trouble, regardless of whether we know the dog or not. For many dog people, having once seen a dog in trouble, we carry its image with us and know that the compassion we feel is irreconcilable with a callous sense of 'reason'. We change our plans, we stop, we help.

Risking life and limb

Is there anyone who hasn't seen a dog wandering in traffic on the freeway or in the city streets? Lost? Abandoned? Many of us feel like Robin, who routinely picks up lost dogs. "If it were my dog out there running around . . . " Robin says, her voice trailing off as she remembers. "A friend's dogs got out one night and ended up on the freeway. One was hit by a car and killed. My friend was devastated. If it were my dogs out there, I'd want somebody to take the effort to try to get them and find their home."

One fall day, Stacey was driving down the freeway in her Jeep with her husband Andrew and her dog Sara, on the way to see her sister run a race. Traffic slowed, stopped, and began backing up. "There was a Rottweiler running down the fast lane," Stacey exclaimed. "I was in my bare feet, but I grabbed Sara's leash, hopped out, and started running, weaving through the cars. The dog turned to face me, frothing at the mouth. For a split second I was afraid, but he was just scared. When I crouched down, he came right over to me and I hooked the leash on. A big eighteen-wheeler held the line as I ran off the freeway, and I heard someone yell, 'Why are you running your dog on the freeway?'" Andrew met Stacey at the bottom of the off-ramp and they took the dog home. "He was very responsive to collar and leash—someone had done work with him. I put an ad in the paper and a man called who had lost a Rottweiler matching this dog's description. The look on his face when he walked through the door was one of such disappointment—it wasn't his dog." Still in college and already having one dog, Stacey couldn't keep this one too, so she brought him to a shelter that didn't euthanize dogs. "As I left, he jumped up, put his paws on the counter, and watched me. I lost it and I bawled—I felt like I was abandoning him. After only two weeks I loved and was attached to him as much as he was to me. Driving back I was stopped for driving forty-five miles an hour in a twenty-five mile-an-hour zone. I don't think the motorcycle cop got one word in because I was crying so hard." Stacey heard later that happily the dog had found a very good new home.

A dog in danger often brings out the best in us. When it's our own dog, the adrenaline can prompt immediate action even where a reasonable caution would otherwise overrule. Nisa and her ex-sled dog Floyd were walking along one day when he and a Rottweiler that lived down the road got into a serious fight. Eventually, the Rottweiler had Floyd down on the ground, clasping his jaw in his mouth. "Floyd let out this dreadful shriek, obviously in pain," Nisa said. "The dog's owner was completely useless; he made very little attempt to separate them." At the time, Nisa was pregnant. Should she interfere? "I was pregnant enough to make me think twice— 'Should I be doing this?' Then I decided, 'I *have* to!' I had all my winter gear on, so I figured if the dog bit me it might go through my mittens, but probably wouldn't get very deep. So I jumped in there, kicked the Rottweiler off my dog, and dragged Floyd home." Later, when she'd calmed down, Nisa reflected on her actions. "It's not something I would normally feel comfortable doing—kicking a dog—but I wasn't going to let him kill my dog. I'm surprised he didn't bite me, actually. It speaks well for the Rottweiler that he didn't turn on me when he was in that kind of blood-lust mood."

And, of course, so many dogs have risked themselves for us, sometimes with an intelligence that seems uncanny. Mike has long loved dogs, although his relationship to animals began as a boy growing up in Kenya, with his pet cheetah. One night Mike was out on his bike with his Doberman, King, at his left side and Boomer, his Lab, at his right, on a six-foot rope with a leash clip at each end. "I was riding up my street on the left-hand side of the road. A truck turned into the street and I figured the guy had seen me. But he came flying around the corner and the next thing I knew I ended up on the ground. I don't remember hitting the ground or anything; I guess I bounced off his hood and landed on my head." The truck driver took off as Mike dazedly got up to check his dogs. He saw Boomer on the sidewalk and King standing in the street. "I started toward King and he was ignoring me, kind of watching the other way. I think with the impact of the hit, he was a little disoriented—I know I was. I got to about fifteen yards from King when another car came at us. I ran toward him, calling, 'King! King!' He turned around and looked at me, then turned back, faced the car, and took a step towards it. He knew I was hurt—I didn't know I was hurt—I was thinking more about him. He just stood his ground to protect me. So he got hit, and, God, I can still see it in my head.

"Boomer got to him before I did. He went over to his buddy and grabbed him by the scruff of the neck and tried to pull King out of the street. I couldn't see the extent of King's injuries, but I knew he was hurt bad, because he wasn't moving, wasn't trying to get up." The second driver also fled the scene. "I'm standing in the middle of the street—covered in his blood and my blood. One of the neighbors brought a blanket and wrapped him until the humane society showed up." At the hospital, Mike learned that King's injuries included severe brain damage. "Putting him down almost killed me. He was my first—all mine—not half my parent's or half my sister's. He's still with me, right here, in my heart." Eventually, another Doberman, Copper, came Mike's way to keep Boomer company. Experiencing the depth of his feeling for King, Mike said, "Life goes on. But not without a dog."

Nothing reveals the strength of the bond between dogs and us as much as the wordless burst of empathy which impels us into action when a dog is in trouble. We leave behind the rational, deliberate process of reasoning because it is too much slower than the knowledge that comes from what we feel. Instead, an instinct to protect and nurture is triggered that we usually reserve for humans, most often family and close friends. That we include our dog among this group is shown by our spontaneous, "unthinking" actions.

Who wants the unwanted?

Jasper was another lucky "freeway dog." Ken found him when he was about ten months old, dumped on a frontage road. Saving him wasn't easy. "I tried approaching him with cookies and dog food, but every time I got close he snarled at me with a wrecking-yard guard dog kind of look," Ken remembered. He called animal control for help and, when they came, was told the dog was across the border in the next county, out of their jurisdiction. "I had to call the pound in that county and then made three or four trips back and forth trying to get someone to come. Finally I gave up, sat down, and told the dog, 'Bite me!' Instead, he put his head on my lap and rolled over." Ken was sitting on the curb with the dog when the local police arrived. "They told me I had to get out of the road or they would arrest me. I told them I was trying to keep the dog from being run over, which might cause an accident. Then a Burl Ives look-alike who worked for the pound in whose jurisdiction we were sitting showed up. The police said the dog had to go to the pound. 'Burl' said, 'Why don't you just let him take the dog? He's got it under control.' So, I brought him home."

That was just the beginning. He and his wife, Julie Schleisser, had to go to work that night. "I put a leash him on to walk him; he curled up in a ball, peed on himself, and wouldn't move. I'm thinking 'What will happen to my leather sofa and cashmere overcoat?' I took all my good clothes, stuck them in the bedroom, closed the door, and said, 'Okay, pal, see you later.' I returned to find diarrhea all over the living room and a trip to the Price Club's worth of toilet paper chewed up. I'd brought back a sandwich in a cellophane wrapper, which he grabbed. 'Give me that,' I said, but he growled and ate the sandwich, wrapper and all. I had a monster dog in my house that I thought would kill me in my sleep." The following morning, Ken left the dog at the pound.

However, having been abandoned as a child, Ken could not live with this decision, so after a bad night, he called the next day to ask whether the dog had been claimed. "'No,' they told me. He had gone totally psychotic, snapping at everyone. 'What do you do with a dog like that?' I asked. They told me they keep them for a week and then they kill them. I thought—and I know this isn't the right thing to do—I'd rather leave him in a state park than send him to Auschwitz." Ken went to visit the dog and was told he was vicious. "I leaned against the chain link and he came up to sniff me. I stuck the arm of the sweatshirt that he'd chewed up the first night into the cage. He pulled it in and rolled over, excited and playful. Clearly, he'd once been abused." Ken visited every day until he brought Jasper home again. Five months would pass before Jasper would tolerate other people. "There were times I wanted to kill this dog," Ken said. "But my life changed as I realized what a little love could do for a totally wild crazy creature. He's turned out to be the best dog I've ever had." A little love is exactly what dogs like Jasper haven't had. And by drawing upon a source of love in ourselves, and extending it to them, we may find our own old wounds healed over at last.

Patrick, who as a child had been badly bitten by a German Shepherd while trying to break up a dogfight, was alarmed by Lady, a wizened, peaceful old German Shepherd, when he encountered her on the street one day. He was reassured by Lady's owner Michael that he had nothing to fear. Then Patrick, a writer, listened with interest while Michael told him how he met Lady. "Years before," Patrick recounted, "Michael had saved her from two men about to destroy her, a rope knotted around her neck, the men whipping her, Lady fighting so hard her neck bled and her body was a mass of bloody slashes. He wrapped her in a blanket, took her home, and put her in the coal cellar where she sat bolt upright with an ugly growl and wouldn't let him near her. To feed her, he had to open the door quickly and shove in the food. His parents thought he was crazy."

Patrick explained that after about six weeks, Michael felt the time was right—he got a plate of food and approached the door. "He opened the door, the first time he'd held it open long enough to let the light in for more than a second. She was a mass of scars. She had her eyes fixed on him real deadly, her teeth clenched. Michael talked to her for about an hour and then shoved the food in. She wouldn't take her eyes off him. So he reached in real slowly, talking to her all the time while she kept up a hideous growl, and patted her lightly on the tip of the nose. They've been good friends ever since."

Hearing the tale of Michael's persistence and Lady's change of heart changed Patrick's perception of them both.

Shortly after Elaine's mother died, a friend brought Elaine a puppy that had been left by the side of the road in a box. Elaine was known for finding homes for strays. "I couldn't believe it," she said. "He looked just like my childhood dog! I thought this was a gift from my mother—Freckles, reincarnated." Her husband was less than thrilled. "When Ed came home and saw him, he wouldn't even speak to me. We were ready for divorce court because I had done it again." Here is another instance of a deep feeling from childhood that emerges to change our present lives for the better.

It took a while for Ed to be won over. He remembers, "I was feeling I wanted to travel more so I didn't want another animal. I didn't want anything to do with the dog. He was very difficult to housebreak—it took about a year, maybe longer." Then Woody ran away. "We woke up at two in the morning, Elaine crying, thinking she heard him barking in the distance. I got up and said, 'Come on, let's go.'"

"It was the first time Ed showed any interest in him," Elaine said. "It was raining and he had his flashlight, calling Woody's name. We didn't find him, but the next day he came back." She laughed, "Now Ed loves Woody more than me."

Lots of people will only adopt the "perfect" dog: the six-month-old housebroken lap-sitter. "Sadly, we get twelve- or thirteen-year-old dogs where the owner has died or gone into a nursing home," explained Mary, a veterinary technician, who started a volunteer Poodle rescue group. "None of the family members want to keep the dog, which may be generally healthy, but less active or losing a little sight. But we have wonderful success stories with generous, loving people who've said, 'I'll give this dog a home.' Some people want their dog put to sleep after they pass away, believing adjustment would be impossible. But the dogs adjust well—in rescue work you see it all the time. Given the right environment, they quickly adapt to a calm routine and gentle handling and speaking."

When a baby arrives, a dog may suddenly be left out in the cold—emotionally as well as physically abandoned. Barbara, who considers her responsibilities to her dog a preview of parenting, has neighbors who haven't done likewise. "Before the neighbors had kids, their dog was their child. Now when they go away for the weekend or on vacation, they leave the dog alone outside with a bag of crumblies. For me, animals are part of the family. Like a first child, the dog will feel jealous for a while when the second arrives, so you have to make sure you're still giving it attention. You don't put the 'first child' out in the yard." Concerned, Barbara suggested their dog come play with hers. "Our dogs get along very well—they love to play. Now, when the neighbors leave town, they come over and tell us. I'll bring their dog over to our house for a few hours every evening, and in the afternoon I'll take her out to play with our dog. Maybe when the newness of their baby wears off, they'll pay their dog more attention."

At the age of eleven, with the support of her mother, Merrill, who is now among the dog people at AutoDesk, went to great lengths to nurse a very sick dog. After searching several weeks in vain for her dog who'd disappeared, she made a last trip to check at a shelter. There she came upon a young Schnauzer being brought in by a family. "They were moving and couldn't take him," she explained. "I looked at him and there was an instant connection. I adopted him that day—unaware he was sick with distemper."

Three different vets told Merrill he needed to be put down. Having lost one dog, she wasn't about to lose another so quickly. "I was young and stubborn: as soon as euthanasia was brought up, I grabbed my dog and walked out the door to find a vet who would help me. I had to give Panky his chance. Being naive helped me—I didn't understand the seriousness of the disease." Her mother patiently took her from vet to vet. "My mom did this for me as well as for the dog. My parents had recently divorced and Panky was my companion to help me through things. She saw how determined I was and she wanted to support me."

Finally, they had some luck. "My fourth vet said we can try . . . and hope. We discovered that the only thing he would eat was chicken liver, so we cooked them for him every day. That turned out to be what he needed to nourish his body and he made it through." It wasn't exactly chicken soup, which is a metaphor for a strong, loving concern that carries the day, but nevertheless it was chicken that did the trick. Panky is now seventeen years old and, although blind, managing very well.

People who come to the rescue of unwanted dogs act from altruism born of a sense of responsibility to this species which has been joined to ours so intimately. Some also feel the dog's plight touching something deep and unresolved in them. Then, as the dogs heal and became part of their lives, that something—whether an unfulfilled need or a hurtful experience—has a chance to be accepted and healed as well.

Emotionally at risk

Sometimes, as with Mike, a dog saves a human from physical harm, but more often they rescue us emotionally. "Dogs saved my life," Elaine maintained. "I was adopted, and always felt I didn't belong anywhere. My parents were first-generation European Holocaust survivors, so we had no relatives. But I always related to animals, and particularly dogs. My dad loved animals and brought dogs home constantly, little puppies for my brother and me. Then the puppies would disappear—my mother would tell us they ran away. My father was crushed. He fell in love with every scroungy little puppy he found at his store." Elaine and her brother learned that their mother abandoned the dogs somewhere while they were in school. "One puppy that we'd had for a week or so walked back from miles away, through freeway traffic. That shocked her mother into thinking she'd better not do it anymore. Then we got Freckles, a black and white little mutt—my best friend." Un-

110

fortunately, Elaine's parents didn't get along, fighting every night. "I could always go to Freckles. He waited for me unconditionally.

"When I was thirteen I got my own room in the basement and Freckles stayed with me. We were inseparable. My mother didn't try to get rid of that dog and she actually grew to like him." After Elaine married, Freckles remained with her father. When her father died, she couldn't take Freckles because dogs weren't allowed in her apartment building. She sneaked him in for a while but then found him a home. "Driving Freckles to his new people, giving them the little Freckles carpet he slept on, his bowl and things, knowing that I was giving him away while he didn't know—it was devastating. But he has a good home. It was the right thing to do."

Jim grew up on a farm where dogs and cats were barnyard animals, not pets, so he never really thought about having one. One day, as he and his wife Heidi were leaving their apartment for work, late because of an argument, the gardener offered them a stray mutt. Jim didn't want it but grudgingly went along with Heidi when she accepted. "Apart from Heidi and me finding each other," Jim said, reflecting on the then undiagnosed depression which had led him into arguments with his wife, "Muffin was probably the best thing that happened to us. He took over our lives—especially mine."

Then Jim and Heidi bought a home and Jim went into business for himself, and they acquired a second dog, Bibi.

"Heidi had a job she hated, working late into the night and early morning. Meanwhile, my business was failing and I was very depressed and angry. I didn't want anybody or anything in my life . . . I didn't want to become attached to anyone or anything, because then if I lost it, it would be too damn painful. When I closed the shop at nine and came home, our daughter was already asleep, so it was like nobody was there except Muffin and Bibi. I'd throw myself on the bed and think, 'Why don't I just end it all? Who cares if I live or die? Who would miss me if I were gone?' Muffin would jump up on the bed, stand by my chest, and look me straight in the eyes as if to say, '*I* would!'" Muffin's affection and love helped sustain Jim through the worst period of his life. "I didn't want anybody or anything in my life—even after I finally allowed a woman into my life . . . I didn't want to become attached to anyone or anything, because then if I lost it, it would be too damn painful. I changed from someone who didn't want a dog in his life to someone who couldn't manage without one."

A mix of unfortunate circumstances—a traumatic encounter, an unhappy relationship, a stressful interval of living alone—can heighten a person's anxieties for an exhaustingly long time. Karen experienced just such a debilitating situation. "My husband was home every night of the seventeen years we were married," Karen began. "One night I woke up to find a burglar in the bedroom of our condo." Immobilized with fear, she watched the burglar rifle both night stands while keeping an eye on her and her husband, who slept through

112

the whole encounter. After that, she never slept well, even with the bedroom door locked and a new burglar alarm turned on. "When we divorced about five years ago, my trouble with sleeping was exacerbated. Because the burglar had woken me at one thirty in the morning, I would fall asleep on the couch with my clothes on. I'd wake up after one thirty or two A.M. to go into the bedroom—after the time the burglar would have been there."

Karen took self-defense classes and kept a canister of pepper spray on her night stand. She knew her fear was disrupting her life, but she became accustomed to living with it, to never having a peaceful night's sleep. One day a friend whose dog had died asked Karen to go with her to look for another. Karen began thinking a dog might help. They went to the pound and then the SPCA. "I spotted a smallish German Shepherd-mix huddling back in a corner and I thought she was beautiful. I wanted a dog I could pick up, for taking to the vet and such, and Comet was the biggest dog I could pick up. I brought her home, even though I didn't yet know if she could bark. After a couple of days, I found out she could.

"She's totally changed my sleeping habits. Almost immediately, I started sleeping in my bedroom again. I don't sleep on the couch anymore, I go directly to bed. I used to leave on three lights outside, three inside, and one in the bedroom. Now I only leave on one outside and inside. I don't lock the bedroom door anymore, I leave it open. If someone comes on the property, she'll let me know." While it's reassuring to know a dog could attack and bite an intruder, it's perhaps more reassuring that Comet is not an inanimate weapon, she's a living being, one who cares, one who attends, and who can restore confidence more than a weapon or self-defense classes.

Dog behavior trainer and breeder, Lynne Crosby recounts, "A relative of mine had been in an accident and suffered a spinal cord injury. There was a possibility Brian would walk again although the doctors were not terribly hopeful. If he was ever going to walk, he had to start his physical therapy as soon as he was healed enough to cope with it. He had a lot of pain, so much that he'd withdrawn from the world. He was thoroughly depressed. He couldn't fathom not being an athlete anymore.

"We had a dog at the time, a Miniature Schnauzer, very active, very cute. Trinket went in and pulled off the blanket that Brian had over his lap. It wasn't a random action—the way she did it she was clearly saying 'Come out and play. Enough of this. Stop feeling sorry for yourself and let's go for a walk.'

"'What are you doing?' he said to the dog. 'I'm cold, I need the blanket. Lynne!' he called. I heard him but didn't go in. He couldn't see me because of the angle of the wheelchair. He got frustrated and mad—it was the first time he'd ever expressed anger at the situation. He yelled at Trinket that he was going to kill her. At that point I said, 'You have a problem.'

"'Get that dog out of here.'

"'The hell with that. You need her a lot more than you need me.' He started to cry. That's when he started to heal."

Brian had had a lot of humans—nurses, therapists, doctors—try to help him. But it was Trinket's lack of a "helping" motive that Brian could accept, and the dog's innocent joy at wanting to play, contrasted so starkly with his anger, that he had to acknowledge it when gently confronted by Lynne.

Never let go of your team

Sometimes it's not easy to tell who is the rescuer, who the rescued. When Paul Scherke first learned about dogsledding, people shared lots of advice with him about the dos and don'ts. "Often, I was told that all the rules in dogsledding boiled down to one—never let go of your sled. No matter what you do, don't fall off that sled, stick with it. If you fall off, the dogs won't hear your commands and they'll just keep on going.

"Early in my mushing career, I was in the forest collecting firewood on a very cold winter day with a powerful ten-dog team. I expected to make a short trip so I was only lightly dressed. I was feeling rather confident on the back of the sled. But then while the dogs were clipping along at a pretty good pace, I got distracted and slipped off the sled. Sure enough, the dogs kept going, the distance between us growing fast. All the screaming and hollering in the world wasn't going to stop those dogs, and try as I might, there was no way I could run fast enough to catch up.

"I knew the road dead-ended at a lake and that if they went on, there was no stopping them. It was well into the evening, dark, and I was in a bit of a panic. I kept running behind them—for miles—hoping that maybe something would distract them or that they'd get caught in a tree or wrapped up somewhere so I could retrieve them. Then the wind came up and it became difficult to detect their tracks in the snow. Sure enough, they went right off the end of the road onto a big frozen wilderness lake that went on for about fifty miles into no-man's land. I trekked out onto the lake in utter desperation; the wind was so strong and it had gotten dark enough that I could barely see their tracks.

"I was just about to turn around when my eye caught a hint of a speck way out on the ice. I didn't recognize it—it was no rock or reef that I knew. On a whim, I thought I'd go out and check. I trudged a few miles out on the ice and was greeted by quite a scene. Sitting all by his lonesome on a bucket was an old fisherman who'd punched a hole in the ice to fish for crappies. Circled around him peering intently down that hole was my team. All ten dogs. The old fellow didn't say anything . He didn't look up until, still playing it pretty straight and without cracking a smile, he said, 'All I want to know is—who's going to pay for my crappies?' My dogs had come careening across that lake, spotted him, and gone detouring over to him. He'd had a pretty good string of frozen crappies surrounding his hole in the ice, but before he knew what was going on, those dogs vacuumed up all the fish and parked around the hole waiting for more.

"It was fortunate that he happened to be out there fishing. It spared me the agony of losing that dog team forever. I gave him a lift back into town on the sled and we joked about that fish story for a long time after. So—never let go of your team!"

CHAPTER NINE

ROUGH PASSAGES

In the difficult are the friendly forces,
the hands that work on us.

Rainer Maria Rilke

One moment the dog is galloping happily across a field, the next moment sprawled on the ground yelping in pain from a torn ligament. We feel awful about Dog's pain, but also about the looming vet bills. Or Dog, no longer a puppy, snarls and won't let us pass in the hall. Or Dog bites the mailman and gets impounded by the police. How do we respond? Do we try to train the dog? Do we get rid of it? The inopportune disasters, the tough decisions forced on us, the boiling over of feelings can drive us to want to give up on a dog, to terminate the difficult situation by severing the bond. But with adversity also comes an appeal to strengths we never knew we had. Employing them, we recognize that how we respond to difficulty is a significant part of what defines us as individuals.

Hard times

Serious illness often strikes like a thunderstorm, intense and frightening. One morning, Lisa noticed that Blarney wasn't feeling well. Later, at the vet, the dog was normal except for a fever, but by the next evening, his fever was higher. "He could barely walk when we took him back to the vet. After doing x-rays, barium, and ultra-sound, they found a partial torsion, where the stomach distends and twists on itself. He had to have emergency surgery the same day." Lisa and her husband, Nick, were afraid they'd lose their dog so they spent the night at the hospital. "We felt traumatized that day; we couldn't go to work, just sat and cried." They telephoned friends who loved Blarney to keep them informed of his condition as they would for any family member. And Lisa discovered just how much Blarney had found a place in Nick's affections. "When the vet told us the treatment would be expensive, my husband, who is always so cost conscious, said 'I don't care if it's twenty-thousand dollars.' I looked at him and said, 'Now I know why I love you.'" Lisa and Nick had definitely expected to feel Blarney's loss strongly at the end of a normal life span. But the sudden, life-threatening illness brought the dreaded pain into the present, and they had a chance to realize just how much they appreciated their dog, with years of life remaining for him.

Unfortunately the outcome isn't always happy. "My sister's first dog," Diana told us, "got into a shopping bag and ate a whole tin of cocoa. The vet said she'd probably be okay if she lasted through the night, but around six in the morning she had a heart attack and died in my sister's arms." The shock of a sudden, unexpected death can leave a lasting mark. "She was so upset that it was a couple of days before she could even call and tell me. Two weeks later, when we were all home for Christmas, she was often in tears. It was devastating for her." As so often happens, Diana could offer only her compassion and presence.

Some difficulties require patience and endurance. "Rescuing Doozie was tough," Nancy Dusseau said. "He'd been mistreated so badly he acquired a lot of behavior problems. His former owner couldn't take care of him and gave him to someone who staked Doozie outside in the back yard where he got no attention and was attacked by neighborhood dogs." By the time Nancy rescued the Soft-Coated Wheaten Terrier (assisted by a breeder), Doozie had been beaten up and abused so much that loud noises, slamming doors, or even angry looks sent him cowering in a corner. He was about ten pounds underweight and wouldn't eat. Then he tried to bite the garbage man. "The breeder wasn't sure whether or not he'd keep biting people. It was pretty serious. For a while I thought I was going to have to put him down—he was too unpredictable. But no matter how hard training him would be, I simply couldn't let him die. Anything short of that was easier."

Since Doozie attacked other dogs, Nancy couldn't bring him to an obedience school. She got some help from a woman at the SPCA who helps turn misbehaving dogs around. The woman coached Nancy on what to do, but seemed very pessimistic about the outcome. Nancy began working with Doozie. "Biting is a split-second instinctual reaction, so I had to restrict him to situations where he had no opportunity to react, not take him places where I couldn't control what happened." Nancy limited Doozie's world for about a year so he wouldn't be bombarded by stimuli he didn't know how to deal with. "I didn't like leaving him at home while I took my other dog for a walk at the beach or the park. Part of me wanted to give him back. At times I thought I wanted to simply get another puppy because retraining Doozie was just too hard. It *was* hard, but it worked. Once I got some weight on him and once he was in a stable environment for a year, he came around just fine. Now he's a sweetheart."

Mismatches

A puppy arrives, and we're full of hope and expectations of warmth and companionship. But sometimes, as this new life blossoms alongside our own, things don't work out. Perhaps we are preoccupied, unable to develop a tight bond. Or our temperaments are too different: we're calm and deliberate while the dog is energetic and impulsive, or the other way around. As with humans, adolescence is a crucial time in a dog's life for establishing emotional relationships. And adolescence can be stormy for dogs, as well.

Dog trainer and breeder Lynne Crosby spoke about the passage from adolescence to adulthood. "Puppies are sweet, puppies are lovely, puppies play. Everybody loves puppies," Lynne pointed out. "The question is whether you can love the adolescent, and in a way that he can understand, that sets boundaries for him so that as he matures, he bonds to you. As a dog becomes an adolescent and an adult, he has different relationships with the puppies from his age cohort than with those from the next breeding year. He expects his people—the ones who love him—to grow just as his age cohort does. If someone continues to act like a puppy, the dog will treat them like a puppy, and no bonded emotional relationship will form.

"Dogs who are mentally strong strive to get their place in the pack, competing with the humans whom they see as puppies of their own age also trying to make a place in the pack. It's not so much a challenge to human authority as it is a normal developmental stage." The person's relationship with the dog must adapt to the adult dog's new relationship with them. "An adolescent dog can have the attitude, 'This is mine and this is yours—and maybe what's yours is mine too!' Or the dog can say, 'It's us and it's the world. That man over there is not our friend. Sure, I'll go up and say hello to him, but he's different—he's not our family.' When the young dog says, 'I'm strong and tough and this is my house and it's going to be mine forever' and the person that he's been reacting to since he was seven weeks old says, 'I love you, I love you, I love you,' the dog usually responds with, 'Okay fine I'll handle everything.' Fortunately, with the majority of dogs, the challenge is direct, and if you simply tell him, 'No. My house. Cut that out. I'm top dog here,' then he'll respond with, 'Oh! Okay. You're in charge. I understand.' Then, as the dog becomes an adult, the more you ask him to do, the tighter the bond becomes."

Difficulties arise when we don't recognize that the cute and carefree puppy we loved is becoming an adult with adult responsibilities, with an adult need for recognition as a property-holder, a dog with an established place in the world. "If you form that bond then, it will be the tightest it can probably ever be. One of the high points of having a dog is their believing with all their heart and soul that you are a special person."

It's hard to establish a happy bond with a new dog when, somewhere inside, you are still attached to a beloved departed dog. Carolyn described herself as having been a "Sheba person" more than a dog person. "We got Sheba when I was seven and she died when I was away for my freshman year at college," Carolyn said. They had palled around her neighborhood, all through junior high and high school. "There must be something about the one you grew up with. You have no idea how close you are, you don't realize it will affect you the rest of your life." Later, as an adult, she tried having another dog. "When I got Ingrid," she explained, "I was trying to regain something, hoping the dog would somehow be Sheba. I assumed Sheba represented how all dogs could be. Ingrid was less affectionate, less trustworthy in some ways, more likely to run off. Sheba could be pretty wild around the house but she could also be quiet. Ingrid was a nervous dog; she barked whenever the doorbell rang. It became horrible. Everybody shouted at the dog to be quiet, then had to be civil at the door. I thought Ingrid and I would connect, but we didn't. I always liked dogs, but I discovered finally that Sheba was the one dog I would ever love."

Mismatches can occur not only when we get a dog at the wrong stage in our lives, but also if we get the wrong breed. Susan always wanted an Irish Wolfhound rather than a Scottie. But she realized she couldn't have one after a breeder informed her of some of the health issues and special requirements involved in having a dog of that size. "If people don't know what they're getting into, the dogs may be abandoned or mistreated," Susan realized.

Representative of many breeders, Lynne Crosby carefully screens out people for whom her Kuvaszes would be a problem. "When I place a puppy, I immediately eliminate about 60 percent or so of the people who call me. They don't need a protective dog like a Kuvasz. I don't care what they say, the dog won't fit their lifestyle. Handling it would be a problem for them. In the case of the other 40 percent who say a protection dog is exactly what they want, that they could certainly handle one, that they've had them all lives, I ask, 'Is this something that you actively want or something that's okay if it happens?' If it's just okay, I given them the names of breeders of other kinds of dogs."

Bitten

Dogs need all their limbs to stand, walk, and run; their paws, toughened from contact with the ground, haven't a fine sense of touch and aren't well-adapted for the coordinated handling of physical objects. But their mouths are very sensitive to touch and are free to pick things up. Is it any wonder that they make so much use of their mouths to communicate? Dogs have a range of mouth gestures: a sensitive clasping with just the lips, a warning snap that touches nothing but air, a nip that shows a puppy it's out of line, a bite to ward off a threat.

Sooner or later, possibly everyone who lives with dogs experiences a bite. Often it's a mistake: a hand or leg is in the way when the dog is aroused by something strongly enough to forget itself. At a big show as a contestant with her English Setter, George, Honey had a run-in with another dog. "A dog broke in and challenged George in order to get to me. George, who was always very protective of me, simply stood his ground in front of me—an English Setter doesn't attack." When the other dog's owner came in behind his dog, Honey proposed that each of them grab their dog at the count of three. "Unfortunately, when I went to grab George, his mouth came down on my hand and he bit me four times before he realized he had my hand in his mouth. The dogs didn't fight— and that was great—but my hand was badly punctured. When George sniffed my hand he started to cry.

Although partly in shock from the bites, Honey knew her dog had made a mistake. "He didn't mean it—it was sort of like a shark in a feeding frenzy and all of a sudden something clicked inside him and he realized he had my hand in his mouth. At that point he absolutely froze so he wouldn't do any more damage. He realized exactly what he was doing and was very ashamed. I just gave him a big hug. It was hard on him—very hard on him." From then on, George sought reassurance from Honey that she loved him as much as always, and a deeper bond developed between them. "He was four years old when that happened; from that day on till he died at about thirteen, anytime he came near that hand, it was as if he was apologizing to me."

Other times, we simply don't know what a dog—ours or another's—considers its territory. Janet had never feared dogs; she always felt she could trust them and there was no dog she couldn't make friends with. Then, "about a year ago out walking Waldo, a neighborhood dog just tore out of its yard and bit my leg. I told the child, a member of the family who owned the dog, 'Get this dog away from me, he just bit me on the leg.' When I looked at the bite at home, I told my husband, 'We need to go tell these people.' When we went back, I showed them my leg and told them they needed to do something. Not that I liked it happening to *me*, but the dog could seriously harm a child. They weren't unnice but they were kind of blasé. But we pursued it. I went to the doctor and a report was filed with the Animal Control Center who had the people quarantine the dog with a vet. I'm sure they were frightened because they didn't know what we might do." The dog has since then been under supervision by its owners, but the incident left more than a physical mark on Janet.

"Now, whenever I see a dog, I wonder if it's going to come after me. I'm way more cautious with strange dogs. It's funny to feel that. It's something I'd never felt before."

On the road toward becoming a veterinarian Natasa spent five summers in a vet clinic but hasn't been bitten. She's very careful and attentive. "Any dog I approach, I always put my hand out, let them smell me first, and right then I know. If they look at me, eyes down and hair standing on end, I don't even try. I figure, that's okay, they don't want to be petted—they're having a bad day. Scared dogs would shiver. They wouldn't growl or try to snap right away, only when touched where it hurt. Then you'd take the proper measures, put on a muzzle."

Grooming dog after dog, Merrill's husband Vincent accepts the occasional bite as part of the territory. "I tell new groomers two facts are inevitable: someday a dog will move around and you'll cut it with your scissors; and you're going to get bit. Usually in my line of work, if you get bitten you've done something a dog didn't want you to do, like cut their toenails. In my case, I'd been warned, but I just wasn't paying enough attention. I don't believe in muzzles, unless the dog is outright vicious. Muzzling isn't very nice—just because a person talks too much doesn't mean you should tape their mouth shut. You can turn some mean ones around if you have enough time—be nice and let them know that grooming doesn't really hurt."

Don't blame the dog!

"When I look back now," Eileen admitted, "I realize what a stupid pet person I've been. Stupid pet people are uneducated about alpha dogs or obedience training. I have a Lhasa Apso, just a little guy you wouldn't think you'd have any trouble with. A friend told me when I first got Dickens to crate-train him. I tried, but he cried and I let him out of jail." Dickens decided he was Eileen's boss and became very protective of her. "He challenged anyone who came to the front door, men in particular. He barked at them at first, and then started to bite, including two of my male friends. I couldn't control him except by picking him up and holding him. He struggled and barked and tried to bite. I didn't realize that I was reinforcing his anxiety by picking him up. I just knew I had a problem." She talked to her partner at their dog grooming salon, who recommended a trainer. "The trainer came to do an in-home evaluation of what Dickens was doing. He asked me if I always let my dog sit on the sofa and I said yes. He asked me if Dickens slept in my bed, and I said yes. He started working with Dickens and in just ten minutes the dog was acting better. I couldn't believe it." Eileen continued with the trainer, learning to set bounds for Dickens. In six weeks, he was on his way to being a well-behaved dog.

From then on, Eileen worked with the trainer on all her dogs. "He didn't really train the dog; he trained me. What really changed was my awareness of what was going on in a dog and in our relationship." Eileen developed a new attitude toward her sister's dog, Ralph, a female dog despite the name. "Ralph was totally neurotic, totally possessive. If she were sitting in our way, we all went around her. None of us would tell her to move, because she wouldn't. Now I know you can't allow that. If you do, then when you need the dog to obey—say it's about to run into traffic and you want it to stop—it won't respond to your command. Your relationship with any dog is better if you are the leader. I wouldn't have believed that a long time ago, but I do now."

If a dog has bitten someone, there are a host of factors to consider before taking the drastic step of putting it to sleep, which should remain only a last resort. "I'd run the gamut," Deborah Jones avows. "I would get a behaviorist involved, use sonic behavior modification if absolutely necessary. Look at the food, the supplements, the environment, the communication. Do some x-rays, run some blood tests. Whatever it takes. At times the blood work will show that they're off physiologically and need help. They aren't being stubborn or obstinate; they have pain. Perhaps a cervical vertebra is out of alignment—that's very painful and they will sometimes react with violence until it's fixed." There have been, however, one or two dogs Deborah encountered in her work who couldn't be helped. "I would say let that poor dog go; he's trapped in that body and unhappy. There is freedom and peace on the other side. It's not a scary thing. It would be much better for them to be there than trapped in a tortured body." But the dog needs help and we shouldn't give up on it too soon.

During her first summer working at the vet's, Natasa experienced her first inappropriate euthanasia. "The vet I worked for was great—he gave me lots of hands-on experience and helped me learn a lot of the technical side of the veterinary profession. On my last day of work, a big, friendly Rottweiler came into the clinic and I was told to hold him. He was licking my face and happy. Then they told me to hold his back end. So I did. I didn't know they were going to euthanize him—he just dropped out. Right away I had tears in my eyes. The technician told me that he had bitten a friend's child." Natasa learned that the child had been playing near the dog's food dish while he was eating. The adults hadn't watched the child or the dog. They simply thought the dog was aggressive and that they should euthanize it. "This dog was probably about three years old and could have been a great dog. It really bothers me when people are irresponsible and don't think about potential situations that might arise. There were very few instances like that one, but it hurt every time." Later in her career, she worked for a vet who wouldn't euthanize a healthy animal. Instead, the vet would tell an owner, "You've got to be kidding. I don't like your attitude or appreciate what you're doing. Get yourself a better attitude and find a way to resolve this situation."

The Rottweiler's family didn't provide the dog with leadership. When a dog doesn't know its place, problems inevitably arise, maintains trainer Lynne Crosby. She said, "They become destructive, noisy, hyperactive. They may succumb to allergies more than if they were in a more secure environment. The difficulty is that most people don't recognize this happening. They see a bad dog. They think the dog understands what he's doing is wrong. He doesn't. He may be eating your ski boots, but all he knows is that when you come into the room, you're going to hit him, or something unpleasant will happen to him. He's afraid. The dog is going through problems in the relationship which you have to recognize and solve to end an unwanted behavior. Some of my dogs—under stress in ways other than our relationship, we'd been showing or whatever—have come home and said, 'That carpet really belongs in about four pieces.' It happens once and then it stops. I'll say, 'Sweetie why in the world did you do that? I just bought that carpet. But okay, you were letting out a bit of stress, a little frustration. I love you anyway, that's all right.'"

We need to remind ourselves, particularly when we feel stressed, that dogs are individuals, like us. "Each one has different needs," Julie Schleisser tells herself. "For instance, Lola—that's my baby—I feel confident I can take care of her. Lola's always right there next to me." Her husband Ken's dog, however, was a rescue dog that had been severely abused. "With Jasper, I feel inadequate because I can't tell what he needs. He's very expressive, talking and growling a lot, but I know there's a lot more going on that I don't understand. And he's independent, he doesn't want to hang out with me the way Lola does. Jasper needs a lot of extra care because he has emotional problems that have scarred him."

Aggressive, threatening dogs are thought of by some people as being wicked or evil; some books on communicating with animals even talk about evil animals. Deborah Jones reflected that in all her years of helping people communicate with animals, "I have never encountered a dog that had a sense of personal power and was using it in an evil way. But I have encountered frightening animals whose fears were being acted out. Aggression always came from a source of pain. Ultimately, from what I have learned from animals, there is just love and fear. They are desperately seeking to get back to their center. They may be acting out horribly but it's a cry for help."

Often, we start out blaming the dog because its behavior is what seems to be the problem; its actions initiated the feelings that welled up in us. On closer examination, we discover hidden factors that contributed to the predicament: the dog has been abused in the past; it's grown into a new developmental stage; we've been lax or giving mixed messages. The dog brings its instincts, intelligence, and willingness to the situation of fitting into an environment shaped by humans. But it needs our leadership to show how to do that. We are Dog's mentor in the ways of the human world.

CHAPTER TEN

UNSPOKEN BONDS

Soul to soul all planes are tied
When Sympathy lies between.

George Nettle

"Communication" derives from the same root meaning as "communion:" a holding in common, a sharing. As such, communication is not merely words—spoken or written— but a resultant state of being in which words, gestures, tones of voice, shades of feeling have left their mark. What people say imparts ideas; how they say it conveys what they feel. Dogs communicate with us in ways analogous to those which people use—gestures with tail or paw or ears, facial expressions, barks of different tones and loudness, licks—except they don't use words. Consequently, much of what they have to speak with us about lives in the world of feeling, which has an intelligence of its own. The bonds between Dog and us are mostly non-verbal, as is much of what means the most to us in our lives with other people. They work hard at trying to explain and reveal themselves to us. We make the effort to listen.

Even when nothing seems to be happening, in silence, hearts connect. Michele felt profoundly moved by the interaction between her friend's son, Jeremy, and Mandog. "Jeremy loves to lie on his stomach with his face two inches away from Mandog's face." she said. "He lies with his chin in his hands staring at the dog and Mandog stares back. They can look at each other for hours. If you ask, 'Jeremy what are you doing?,' he'll say, 'Just looking at the dog.'

"'Don't get so close to him. He doesn't want you in his face.'

"'No, he doesn't mind.'

"I'll think the dog is going to take a swat at him, but the dog doesn't seem to care. Jeremy seems to find it very soothing. Whatever they're about, he and the dog seem to know. When they are done, one of them gets up. Sometimes it's the dog, sometimes it's the child. It's a silent communion."

Every dog person has had the experience of being warned of a threat unknown to us but perceived by Dog. As an essential service dogs render us, it's one type of communication we listen for and always heed. As Julie puts it, "Dogs operate on another level. I'd been in my new house maybe a month when Maggie ran over to the door and started to growl—not her possum or raccoon growl—this was something different. Sure enough, someone knocked on the door and it was an unkempt, scary looking man who was clearly high on drugs. He wanted money. My dog was just beside herself. I'd never seen her that way with anyone, nor have I seen her that way since. She wanted that guy out of there and she wanted me to know." Julie believes dogs are always listening to us as well and that we ought not to forget their presence. "Maybe they choose not to communicate with us all the time, but that doesn't mean that they don't know what's being said. For instance, I'm annoyed when people laugh at my dog or make fun of her. It bothers me because I know it bothers her. It hurts her feelings."

Preoccupied with "more important" concerns, we can forget that our dog isn't just acting foolishly or randomly. "Once, when my Kerry Terrier was young and I had some Kerry people at my house, there was a knock on the door," Nancy Han remembered. "When I opened it, the dog—who'd never acted like this before—lunged at this guy, growling. It scared him to death. The guy jumped back, held up his hands, and said, 'I must have the wrong house.' I apologized to my guests—I was very embarrassed at my dog acting like this. Some Kerries can be really rowdy and I didn't want my dog to get that label. A little later, the dog went out the doggy door and started barking like a maniac in the backyard." Nancy again felt embarrassed and put the dog in his crate. "When my guests got up to leave, we went out the front door and found four police cars. An officer told me a burglar had broken into the house next door. But someone was home who called 911, and the police came with a K-9 unit. My dog knew the guy was bad when he came to the house. When my dog was making a ruckus in the yard, he was helping the police dog. I went from totally embarrassed by his behavior to very proud."

For the most part, however, Nancy listens to her dog, especially when he wants to show her things. "I had a cat that loved birds. I don't know why, but wild birds would come and sit around her and she just sat there. She'd come in the doggy door with a bird in her mouth and the bird would fly out, unhurt. One day my male Kerry kept jumping on me until I paid attention. He led me upstairs. When I got up there, he was lying down with a bird between his feet. He wanted to show me the bird needed to be let back outside. He was always telling me things like that."

Understanding their dogs runs in Bonnie Moore's family. Bonnie's mother feeds walnuts to the squirrels in her yard. "But she can't put the nuts out because of a large bully bird who controls the area," Bonnie explained. "Her dog, Scotty, watches for the squirrels, who run up and down the fence when the bird is gone. Scotty will then go get Mother and say, 'They're here, you need to go take them some food.' He'll run to where she keeps the nuts and then he'll run back over to the door. He really looks after the squirrels—he wants her to feed them!" Bonnie understood the barks of her own dog, Taffy. "I knew when she was warning me of danger and when she was just barking at people passing by. I knew when she was chastising her daughter, Ebony—she used a different bark. When I heard her do that, I'd stop her. And when she heard me chastising Ebony, she'd stop me. So the three of us had an understanding type of relationship."

Lady was also a good watchdog, barking alerts when someone came onto Deborah Jacobs' porch. "I trusted her discrimination—I could tell by her bark whether the visitor was a friend, acquaintance, or stranger. Lady was so eager to greet visitors that many times I opened the door with one hand while holding her back by the collar with the other. If I didn't feel comfortable with a stranger at the door, I let them see more of Lady lunging forward trying to get out and this always made them back off. What they couldn't see—hidden behind the door—was Lady's tail wagging like crazy."

Preparing her dogs for a show about five hundred miles away, Honey bathed them before putting them in her van. "My English Setter, Lisa, who had long since stopped being shown, came out and looked in the van. I looked at her and said, 'No, Lisa, you can't go.' She looked at the van and looked back at me and I said, 'I got a deal for you—go into that van, and if you can find a place for your crate, you can go.' She immediately got into the van behind the driver's seat where there was a crate, got on top of the crate, and sat there and looked at me, knowing her crate would fit there. I said, 'Okay, fine, you win.' If you talk to each dog as an individual and they're around you enough, they understand what you're doing, your tone of voice, and your mood swings."

Deborah Jones calls her specialty non-verbal communication. "I try to be very practical in the help that I give." For the most part, the exchange takes the form of mental images, physical sensations, emotions. On rare occasions, she has "heard" a word. "I was working with a dog who was barking excessively. At one point, the owner asked me if the dog liked his name. Would he like a different name?" The dog had been adopted from the pound and the owner was curious whether the dog might have a preference. "Clear and loud as a bell I heard the name 'Rocky.' So I said to the man, 'Well, he likes the name Rocky.' My client said, 'Sure he would. My dad's dog's name is Rocky and this dog would love to be my dad's dog— he adores my dad.' I was so in awe that I didn't even hear the man's next question."

The variety of things animals convey is astonishing. We're all familiar with a warning bark, an appraisal of a stranger. But listening closely opened each person to a wider range of communications. Dogs expressed their preferences, told what they'd like to be called, acted as intermediaries for other animals, mediated disputes. When we assume their actions to be meaningful rather than random, communication begins.

Touch

Physical contact is the most direct form of communication. Touch is intimate and powerful. As a bodyworker, Lynn Vaughan has a highly developed sense of touch. Her vocation was inspired by childhood experiences with her grandmother. "She was very special in my life," Lynn said, "the earliest influence I can think of that led me to what I'm doing now. Like a tiny bird, she weighed maybe ninety pounds, and she had tender hands. Very gently, she'd lay them against an animal's head or neck, usually a dog, and I'd watch the dog melt under her touch. It was such a beautiful sight. For my grandmother to have that kind of touch and awareness aroused my curiosity." As Lynn grew up, she tried to touch dogs and other animals as her grandmother had. "It occurred to me a only few years ago, when she was about eighty, to ask her if she had an intention. She was touching my dog Heather at the moment and she said simply, 'Well, I like to feel the subtle changes that happen under a light touch.'" Her grandmother's statement confirmed Lynn's own experience, that a light, soft touching revealed more than a heavier one.

Deborah Jacobs saw that Lady communicated with all the household beings through touching. "When the time had come for my cat Ozzie, who was dying of cancer, I took him to our other two cats and to Lady to say good-bye. They touched noses, every single one of them. But it was more than that. They seemed to touch each other emotionally. Lady raised her nose two or three times as if she was sniffing the air at me, towards my face. Then she looked down at Ozzie and rubbed her nose on the top of his nose, and pulled back a bit. Then she rubbed her nose over his back legs. Then she sat, with that calm, centered look she gets. Ozzie was very receptive, although previously he and Lady had kept their distance. But this was particularly loving and accepting, and seemed to be a good-bye. I felt reassured when I saw it. At the veterinary clinic, I made it real clear that even though they had their own routine, I was going to hold Ozzie as he died. I feel that I was matching the sense of the other animals when I was doing that. They helped me and guided me. That was the first time I had ever been close to death in that way."

We touch our dogs and are touched by them so frequently, so unself-consciously, that touch becomes a natural place to begin developing our sensitivity to what they are communicating.

Two become one

Perhaps no pair is closer or has a need to communicate as well and truly as do a blind person and a guide dog. As Morgan Watkins describes his experience, the boundary between dog and human blurs and becomes permeable. "I've gone from having blue eyes to having big, beautiful brown eyes. When I'm moving, it's as though I see again because the connection between us has become so smooth. He's given me agility I thought I lost years ago—moving through crowds, not bumping into trash cans, things like that. Do you really think about looking to your left or right when you walk down the sidewalk? No, you just do it. It's below consciousness. When you're working with a guide dog, when it's synched up, you move like that—there's no conscious control."

Morgan sensitively described what may be possible for all of us if we put in the time and make the effort. "With very little work and few gestures, he picks up on me and I on him.

When he halts or twists around, I just do that without thinking about it. Sure, if I thought about it, I'd realize that my left hand is in the handle, I'd become aware that there are two entities—but who cares? We have that connection. Sometimes when we're working, it's hard to distinguish where I end and where dog begins—a really strange sensation when it first clicked. Too bad people can't try out a guide dog just to see what it's like." Ever since he was a boy, Morgan liked dogs, but didn't really know the mind of any dog before Fantom. "I've become very aware of who he is and how much he understands, what he can think through, what things make him nervous, how he reacts to my moods, when he needs love, when he needs encouragement. It wasn't until Fantom that I realized that what makes a dog joyous and happy is what makes you joyous and happy."

Communing with a dog can bring a balance, evening the highs and lows, as if pouring energy from one of us to the other until we both are filled equally. "Dogs have a knack for absorbing what's going on near them," said Allan. "When our kids are stressed, or when school is getting on their minds, they go over to the dogs, lie down on the floor, and spend some time petting and communicating with them. The dogs absorb whatever is going on and seem to give back strength. And, when you know and appreciate a dog, you can feel exactly what's going on in their lives, too. Somehow. It's not one-way."

A dog may experience the bond with a person as one so

overwhelmingly close that the dog may not survive an enforced separation. "In 1986," Paul Scherke began, "We were eight people with five teams of sled dogs planning an expedition across the Arctic Ocean to reach the North Pole." Their trip was destined to become the first confirmed trek to the North Pole without resupply or outside support. One team member from Alaska raised and trained his own dogs, and had a very tight relationship with his lead dog. "About a month into the expedition, Bob was driving his sled so single-mindedly that he was unaware that the bottom of his mukluks had abraded through on the rough ice of the ocean. He found himself in the tent that night with solidly frozen feet." If he weren't evacuated he risked losing his feet, so an airlift was arranged. "Bob insisted that our only chance for reaching the Pole was if he left his dog team behind for us. We were very grateful, especially because the team was so exceptional.

But with Bob's departure, something happened that none of us had anticipated—his lead dog went into a noticeable slump that worsened steadily over the next few days. The dog's spirit was just gone, and with it his resistance to the cold. Within three days, a dog that had been the leader of the pack, brimming with energy, had to ride on the sled, limp and semi-comatose. We tried to feed him warm broth to bring him around, but he just shut down and quit. The life force went out of him and he soon died. We buried him out there on the ocean ice. He was the only dog we lost on the trip."

Now I get it!

Some people have more of an ability to communicate with animals than others, everyone's sensitivities having developed in different directions. An increasing number of people, however, specialize in communicating with animals, as Deborah Jones and Lynn Vaughan have done. They put a lot of effort into confirming these communications, honing intuition into a reliable instrument. "We all have the ability to communicate with animals non-verbally," maintains Lynn, who does bodywork with animals. "I tend to be a very active, busy person, and my mind works quickly. When I started, I had to learn how to clear my mind and center myself. 'Centered' meant being quiet, emptying my mind, and being aware of my breath. Then I would be ready to listen for whatever is communicated."

Many people feel that they have an intuitive communication with their dog. "Most people are very open," Deborah said. "They just aren't conscious of it. They follow their urges, but they aren't sure if they're right or where the urges come from. The person thinks, 'I'm just feeling that myself, that's what I want to feel.' Without their being conscious of it, the animal still gets through. It's so simple, it's hard."

When we first try to "hear" what our dogs may be telling us, we need to trust our intuition but practice a lot and in situations where what we "hear" can be confirmed. Deborah says, "Often, it's hardest to do with your own animals, so practice on your friend's animals. It makes a big difference."

Deborah also thinks dogs communicate with one

another and with us through images. "We humans have learned a language that has abstract concepts: negatives such as 'don't', 'shouldn't', 'can't'. We'll say things like, 'Don't jump on the couch.' But the picture that they'll see is one of jumping on the couch because there's no picture for the word 'don't'. So they jump on the couch, get yelled at, get very anxious, and start to shut the communication down themselves. It becomes just too confusing to them."

When Lynn is doing bodywork with an animal, she says, "I may find areas of discomfort or sensitivity which would lead me to suspect an underlying medical problem. I then recommend that the person consult with their vet. A proper vet diagnosis should come first, so that what may turn out to be critical time isn't wasted."

Learning to recognize Patch's signals has in turn helped Adam be much more sensitive to non-verbal signals from humans. "As a psychologist, how Patch communicates his state of mind has interested me. When I go to the front door, he communicates his expectation that I'm going to take him on a walk by coming to the door and prancing around, looking excited. Often the first alert I get that somebody's coming to the house is his bark or him stirring and trotting to the door. I can sometimes recognize who is coming to the door by the amount of excitement or arousal he shows, or whether he barks or not; it all tells me whether it's a member of the family, someone he knows, or a stranger. I can also read his other signals, like when he needs to go out, or when he's hungry. When I'm paying attention, he communicates very effectively. It's tuned me in much more to non-verbal signals with people. Now, even in spoken communications, I get more from the tone and inflection of someone's voice."

Mary, the veterinary technician, came home one night from her job not feeling well and got right into a hot tub. "I asked my husband to fix the dog's dinner. Maddie looked a little off—she's always had a sensitive stomach and sometimes won't want to eat. I told Tom to feed her right away. I slithered out of the tub and got in bed. Maddie came to me, stood by the bed, and went 'Woof.' I groaned but asked, 'What's the matter, Maddie?' I got out of bed and she ran to the kitchen to the microwave oven and woofed again, looking me right in the eye. I asked, 'Do you want a potato?' (When her stomach's upset, I often microwave a potato and mash it up with cottage cheese for her.) She started jumping all around, so I put the potato in, went back to bed, and had Tom finish preparing it. She wolfed it down and then brought three toys up into the bedroom, as if to say, 'That's exactly what I needed.'" Familiarity with her dog, taking a "woof" as meaningful, being willing to be guided by her dog's behavior, and above all, paying attention— all added up to "hearing" and understanding.

Hearing always precedes understanding, yet can be the most difficult part for us humans. To make sense of what our dogs are telling us, we must learn to "hear" with our eyes and fingers, hearts and minds, as well as with our ears. The result of this effort is a deeper bond. What has been unspoken does not go unheard.

CHAPTER ELEVEN

THE VENERABLE DOG

Though past youth's active season,
Even life itself was comfort.

Robert Southey

Two A.M. We are awakened, eyes open in the dark, aroused by a bark from downstairs. Dog is fourteen and having a rough night. Our body still more asleep than awake, the air outside the covers chilly, the cozy warmth tempts a return to peaceful slumber. Another bark, this time the pitch a little higher. No thinking, no stalling—turn back the covers, sit up and slide the feet onto the floor (Oh, that's cold!), and struggle into clothing. Go downstairs, snap on dog's leash and guide him slowly out for an emergency walk.

At first it was hard to get out of bed. Then it becomes routine, unquestioned. Dog, ever vigilant, ever watchful, energetic companion for so long a time, now needs our vigilance and tender care. Dog has grown old. Buoyed by advances in diet and veterinary medicine, dogs live as much as half again as long as they once did. Now, many of us will live through a geriatric stage with them. That bundle of furry life and love is a long-term commitment—not a popular concept in these days of disposable-everythings and lust for the latest model of whatever.

As with dying and death, the aging process has been lost from the experience of many people, hidden behind the doors of nursing homes or hospitals, out of sight, out of mind, and very definitely out of our homes. Our dogs give us a chance to learn what's ahead and how to accept and live with it.

Healthy pensioners

A dog may slide into old age gradually, almost imperceptibly, or may skid in with a few jarring ratchets that make us sit up and take notice. Either way, we need to accept and accommodate ourselves to the changes in order to enjoy the remaining years of companionship. "My dog Ttaka is fourteen and there are some tough things about that," Melissa realized. "She's getting arthritic and losing her hearing and sight—I can see it, hear it, and feel it while we're doing things. I'm reminded that she's not going to be around forever." Melissa has adapted to the changes, gradually. "Ttaka's getting pickier about what she eats and how much—or if she's going to eat at all! If she doesn't eat, then I know she won't stay nourished and strong, so I'm forced to get creative with presenting food that's good for her." And taking trips is no longer a spur-of-the-moment event. "It had been fine to leave her with friends when she was younger, but now, what I do for her is beyond what I could count on from others if I went away. On New Year's Eve I thought she'd like me to be around, so I stayed with her even though she didn't realize I opted to stay over going out." Actively seeking ways to accommodate aging bodies can prolong old pleasures. "Ttaka began to miss when she tried to jump on the bed. Her rear quarters are stiff, and she's getting cataracts so her depth perception is off a little. I had a brainstorm one day: I decided to lower the bed. Even though I'd like it to be higher, she's my girl. I took the bed off its frame so it's only two feet off the ground. Now Ttaka never misses when she jumps up. It boosts her confidence."

"I see her contemplating almost everything she does," Melissa said. "Sometimes she just stops and looks as though she's thinking deep thoughts about whether to jump on the couch or not." At times, Ttaka even seems to fall asleep standing up. It frightened Melissa until she realized she could simply help Ttaka lie down. "It's hard when you see them acting older because you don't always know what to do for them—whether some tests are warranted or whether it's the beginning of the end. I took a course in animal communication. I want her to be able to tell me when it's time to let go, rather than going to the vet to find out."

Living with a geriatric dog—or human—is in some ways like living with a baby. Deborah Jacobs has long passed the baby stage with her three children and now cares for Lady, who has just turned fourteen. "When my kids were small I thought it was great when we went on a schedule, but then a few days later the schedule didn't work anymore. Same now with my dog. Lady's skin problems will be doing great, so I think what I've been doing is finally working . . . and then it doesn't work; something else pops up. It's a challenge. I spend more time and money than I ever thought I would, but it's time and money well spent." Deborah remembers thinking, when her daughter first got Lady, that Katy would grow up and leave home to follow her star, Lady remaining at home with her. "Now that we're going through the geriatric phase, I remember what I thought back then, but I had no idea what it meant, how challenging old age would be. When I was a kid, I had two dogs that I loved who died, but it was sudden and it wasn't old age. As a child I heard the phrase, 'Putting it out of its misery.' As a child it seemed so simple. A dog got to a certain age, had this or that trouble, and you 'put it out of its misery.' Now I see there are all kinds of miseries and all kinds of things that can be done about some of them."

Heidi's mother has Alzheimer's. For as long as possible, she lived in a retirement community where she was able to be on her own and keep her dog—it was so important a companion. Then her Alzheimer's worsened to the point where she could no longer care for the dog. She went into a nursing home while Heidi took the fifteen-year-old Cockapoo, Molly. "Mother had Molly since she was a puppy. They've been so close," Heidi said. "The only thing that seems to cause my mother any pain is missing the dog. But even though Mother knows she misses Molly, she can't tell Molly and our Scottie apart—and they look nothing alike. It's been difficult for Molly, too. We took her to visit Mother at the nursing home and as soon as Molly got out of the car, she cried for fifteen minutes. It was awful. Now we bring Mother to our house. The first couple of times, Molly was sad when Mother left. More recently, the past few times, when my Mother comes in Molly gives her a nice big greeting and then stays away. It's almost as if she doesn't want to be hurt."

Adopting her mother's dog has been difficult and painful for Heidi. "We've had Molly about six months and I wasn't able to show her any affection until just recently—I couldn't let her into my heart. My father died when I was a baby and now, although my mother is still alive, she's basically gone." In effect, Heidi was grieving. "Molly's presence shoved that fact in my face: the reason *you're* here is because I've lost my mom. There was nothing Molly could do that I found endearing, and that's not like me; I think all dogs are fabulous. Little things would drive me up a wall, like her constant sniffing on the ground for food. Finally, I had to have a little talk with myself, telling myself, 'If my eyes and hearing were as bad as Molly's, what would be left but my nose and my mouth?' So, I made peace with her."

Heidi's generosity and compassion for human and animal alike have left her open to a bittersweet realization. "A week or so ago, Molly did something cute and I had a spontaneous feeling for her. It's coming in little ways—not all the way yet. But she's also fifteen and not the healthiest animal in the world. It seems to have come full circle. I hated having that dog in my life but now I'm thinking 'I'm going to get invested in this dog and then lose her?'"

A seeing-eye person

Blindness, deafness, or both often accompany old age. Neither one is a mandate for euthanasia. Dogs adapt to the loss of these senses better than most humans do, and with a little help can continue enjoying life. Yoda, the dog who helped rehabilitate the homeless man, lost his vision when he got older. Nancy Duff had the love and patience to care for her geriatric dog. "He started running into things, like trash cans, so I began using a leash all the time. After a while, I realized I was starting to pull him around by the neck because he really couldn't see anything. I got him one of those body harnesses. He took a few days to get used to it, but I had something to grab onto to lift him up a step or over obstacles." In order to get Yoda through the night, she had to get up at three A.M. and lead him into the yard. "It was like having a baby. When he started pacing, it was the two-minute warning to take him down. That went on for about two years. A long time. Towards the end I was really sleep-deprived. Some months after he died, I woke up one morning thinking, 'Wow, I slept all night!'"

"Caring for Panky takes extra effort," avowed Merrill, speaking of her aged dog. "But he's happy and he's well worth it. The furniture has to stay put because he has everything memorized. Most people don't realize he's blind when he's in his house. We mounted a jingle bell on the front door and a cow bell on the back door so he can tell the difference between them. Our six-year-old Pomeranian leads Panky around by the tone of his bark. I love to watch that."

When her English Setter Lisa was going blind, Honey made the mistake of rearranging the furniture in her living room. "She went in and then started crying. I thought, 'What happened?' Well, there was a chair where there'd never been a chair before. I never realized she knew where everything was. I apologized to her and moved everything back." Honey discovered an unanticipated benefit of keeping an old dog company. "Old age is about the only time you can put a Setter in the front yard and know they're not going to run away! They're content just to sit beside you while you garden rather than taking off after every bird. I think the birds know it, too; they don't fly away."

Coping with decline

No matter how well we take care of old dogs, all their functions slow down and old immune systems are subject to bouts of illness. Their eyes fail. Hips become stiff and hind legs weaken. Digestive systems become fragile. Their frailties test our mettle as nothing else does. Old Yoda not only went blind and deaf, but also became completely incontinent. As have so many dog people, Nancy Duff discovered a capacity for patience and an acceptance of the daily disruptions to her life. "I was cleaning up after him three and four times a day," Nancy remembered. "He was really embarrassed about that. Next to being blind and deaf, the incontinence was the hardest thing to bear. Sometimes it got to be a bit much; I'd clean up and ten minutes later have to do it again. But it was also interesting—no matter what he did, my feeling was very calm. I'd just get up and clean it up. I was never angry with him."

Some behaviors of old dogs are mysteries. "Yoda started pacing. He'd sleep all day then around five P.M. he'd begin pacing for hours. I don't know why he did it, the vet didn't know why, but it seems to be common. He still looked pretty good, and he could still walk and get up and down, but he was so bewildered all the time; he wasn't the same dog anymore." Through her experience caring for Yoda, Nancy came to an understanding of readiness for death. "By the time we die, most people, even if they still have their minds, are only a shell of their former selves. The quality of life has diminished so much that it's time to recycle the suit. You've worn it out and it's time to go on."

A number of years ago, before Heidi took in her mother's dog, her own dog Muffin died, and then her other dog, Bibi, had a seizure in the middle of the night on Christmas Eve. "We thought she was dying, but it turned out to be only the beginning of a number of seizures, and she eventually became incontinent." Even though Bibi had a heart problem and a bladder problem, Heidi couldn't let her go so soon after loosing Muffin. "It was just too much. We bought little disposable baby diapers. We put a halter on her and cut a hole out for her tail and pinned the diapers to her halter." Bibi did fine.

So did Bosco, Lee's sixteen-year-old Malamute, who is

incontinent and has to go every hour. Lee tried putting her in the basement at night, but she howled from loneliness. So Lee put her in the kitchen and lined the floor with newspaper. "At first, she was embarrassed and would slink away when I cleaned the floor in the morning. Now she stands watching and says 'Over there—you missed a spot!'"

When Rob's dog Sheba was about ten, she got to the point on walks where she'd sit down because she couldn't support her weight any more. Rob was concerned that he'd have to put her down. "I guess because of my conventional biology background, that was the only thing I assumed could be done," Rob explained. In the labs, animals were routinely disposed of when they had served their purpose. "I didn't think there was any choice. I'd been through it before and I didn't like it, but Sheba was different because she wasn't really sick. Aside from being crippled, she had all her faculties and she was enjoying her life.

"What really decided me on doing something happened after the vet told me that I'd better get prepared to put her down. I lived in an apartment—up two flights of twelve steps and a landing between. I had to carry Sheba up—and she was an eighty-pound dog. One day, I was bringing home some groceries and I left her outside on the grass while I put them away. I figured I'd let her have a little air. The yard was fenced in, it was a nice warm day, and I knew nothing could happen to her.

"A few minutes later I heard a scratching at the door. I

opened it and there she was. Even though she could barely walk, she'd come all the way up the twenty-four steps and the landing. When I saw that I thought, 'God, I have to do something. If the dog can do this, then I can do whatever I need to do.'" Rob consulted a neurological specialist, tried acupuncture, got a K-9 cart to take the dog on walks, had Sheba massaged, and learned to massage her himself. "I was willing to try anything," he said. "I never really made a conscious decision to do this or to do that—I dealt with each crisis as it came. If I'd known beforehand all that I would have to do, my decision might have been different. I would never have believed I could do some of the things I did to help her." All the while, Rob fought a battle about whether he was doing right or wrong. "A lot of people said I was being selfish, that I should let her go. I went to about four different specialists, just to make sure I wasn't. I knew that she still wanted to be here and she was still trying. That's what amazed me—how hard she tried. There were times in my life I tried hard, but when I really think about it I realize I could have tried a little harder. With her there was no hesitation, no half effort. We can all learn from that."

Adapting to the rhythm of an old dog requires patience. Creaky bones need more time to warm up and get going and when they do they never approach the pace of youth. Slowing ourselves down to walk an old dog can open up a new world of impressions. Where once we rushed past the familiar signposts that marked a route taken a thousand times, now we savor them in finer detail, see a thousand things we never saw. One day an empty patch of ground sprouts green. The next day it has grown an inch. Another day, another inch; day by day developing into a tall, sturdy weed with spiky leaves; purple flowers blossom, shine, then fade, petals disappearing one by one; the stem droops, withers, drops to the ground, dry and brown, crumbles, decays. The wind has scattered the debris, the ground is bare again.

CHAPTER TWELVE

THEY LEAVE TOO SOON

When you remember someone, they don't die.
They live in you.

Sunyata

Because our dogs complete their life cycle in so much shorter a time than we do, we may go through the process of death and grieving for a pet several times. For most of us, the facts of death are immediate and unavoidable; there are no nursing homes or hospices for dogs, so they often die in our arms. From this physical intimacy, an opportunity arises for participating simply and directly in a great mystery; whereas our human families are often dispersed, and sometimes estranged, our dogs have nowhere to go but home.

Preparing to say good-bye

Most of us are understandably reluctant to speak of death and dying when we can't anticipate what the effect of broaching the subject might have—rousing painful memories and feelings of hurt or loss, rejection of the speaker. Henry remembers when he was a child coming home one day to find Spot's bed empty. "Aged and infirm, she'd been put to sleep by my parents without their saying anything about it beforehand. I didn't realize until later that my feelings of sadness had been layered over by feelings of hurt and anger. I think my parents wanted to protect me, but my grieving got sidelined for a time, making it more difficult to complete."

Most often, it's better to prepare someone else, and ready ourselves to accept and respond with compassion to whatever comes up. When Michael's childhood dog Pepper had to be euthanized, his parents told him what was going to happen. "They answered questions and talked through the issues concerning death even though they weren't as 'touchy-feely' as some of my friends' parents. Even so, they didn't just put the animals to sleep without us understanding it. My father is a scientist and at an early age we understood what was going on technically—organs and how they work, physiology. It all made sense to us. It wasn't out of the blue."

There is no right or wrong way to experience the end of a life. Elaine loved her dogs, but felt relieved that she and her husband have "managed to escape the deaths of all the pets we've had so far. We haven't had to see them die or bury them. When I couldn't keep Freckles and gave him to his new family, he was already an old guy; it spared me from having him die on me. I was secretly glad to have someone else deal with his death." Freddi, on the other hand, who once raised Scotties, felt bad about not being able to remain with her dogs at the end. "I've had two dogs euthanized," she said. "I wouldn't be any help to the dog. It would be worse with me there—they understand your feelings. I'm crying right now as if I were putting a dog down. I've read about people who held their dog, but I just don't know if I'm capable of doing that. I can make the decision but I can't be there. I doubt that the benefit of having me there would offset the stress I'd convey to the dog." Freddi's concern was about possibly upsetting the dogs, not about avoiding unpleasantness. She'd endured very unpleasant times sitting up nights with one dog who had tumors in her nasal cavities that ruptured when she sneezed, spraying blood everywhere. Freddi held and comforted her while it happened. Neither chemotherapy nor radiation would help, so finally, "it was better to give her a peaceful ending than to have her go on and continue in pain. The vet said, 'You'll know when the time comes to let her go.'" Speaking for many of us, Freddi added, "It's so much easier to talk about it or to make the decision intellectually than it is emotionally."

Letting go is often the hardest part of saying good-bye. Dog is weak or ill—the end is near—but we want another day, another hour of the living presence of this being. Heidi felt she couldn't bear to let Muffin go. "Blind and deaf and weakened, even a slight breeze could topple him. We kept him around much longer than we should have. He went really fast, but it was the hardest thing I think either of us has ever done. We held him as he died."

Sometimes we cling to a desperate hope. Having come to the decision to euthanize her dog, Nancy Han brought him to the clinic. While she was waiting for the vet, a student working at the clinic asked if she could help. "I told her I preferred the vet because it wasn't an ordinary visit," Nancy recounted. "'Are you sure you need to do that?' the student asked. She took the dog's temperature and suggested I leave him overnight so they could try to save him. I left him in the hospital and went home feeling hopeful that he would be young and healthy again. He died there overnight. I was furious, because I knew it was time and I wanted to be with him. I let the student convince me she could save my dog. She didn't mean any harm—she was honestly trying to help him, but it wasn't the way I wanted it to go."

In eighteen years of mushing sled dogs, Paul Scherke never once euthanized a dog because it wasn't performing to someone's expectations. So he found it very difficult to face the day he had to put down the last of the dogs he'd bought from an Eskimo family. "He was my original connection to the world of the Arctic and the far North," Paul explained. "We'd shared many miles together. At sixteen-years old, he couldn't stand any more—not a happy animal. I dreaded the day he would pass, and finally the staff here begged me to put him out of his misery. It was clearly time to let him go, but it was hard to do."

We can learn many things from accompanying another being through the final stages of a life. "It is a precious, emotional time when people's hearts can open," Lynn Vaughan reflected. "I think that's the pain some people try to avoid—it feels like more than they can bear. If a person gets beyond that, and if they have a support system—maybe their vet clinic helping them hang in longer with the animal or perhaps getting more help at home—they can learn a different level of love. Everything is so much more present when mortality is looking us right in the face. We don't know exactly when it's going to happen, but it is going to happen. Feelings for the animal are at an exquisite pitch as you relive memories and sum up the relationship. If you find a way to express those feelings, that in itself is heart-opening. People sometimes reach depths of compassion they never knew they had."

Deciding to euthanize

Quality of life is the key element in deciding over life or death, whether for human or dog. Modern medicine can prolong a human life far past the point when the person wishes to continue living, and increasingly the same can be done for dogs. But whereas humans can make their wishes known, preferably well before the last days, dogs cannot. When they are ill or terribly infirm, we must decide for them.

"Leo was sick for four or five months with stomach cancer and deteriorated quickly in the last month," Angie said. "By the last couple of days, my husband and I realized he was dying. Even on the last day, though, with him at the vet on an I.V., I thought we could prolong his life somehow. But when I said good-bye to him, I realized it would be cruel to keep him going because he was in pain. I couldn't bring him home and then have the same thing happen a day or two later. I told the vet I thought we should put Leo to sleep that day. Had we not done it, it would have been only for our sakes—that we couldn't bear to part with him—not for the dog's."

When the time came for Yoda to die, Nancy Duff suffered a few false starts. "I felt I needed to make the decision and take him in the same day," she said. "Thinking about it overnight was too hard—I'd wake up in the morning and not be able to go through with it." One day, she gathered four friends and took Yoda to the vet. "Yoda got up on the table, lay down, and put his head on his legs. This was very uncharacteristic of him, he was usually nervous at the vet—not outrageously so, but he knew where he was, even the last few times. So, he just lay down that one time and she gave him the shot.

"I'd seen animals die before, but this was the first time I knew it was going to happen. To watch something that is living all of a sudden be not living is a very strange experience. You could just see the life force or spirit leave Yoda. He was peaceful and not fighting it, and wasn't afraid of it. He was tired and it was time. Sixteen and a half for a dog is a long time. He didn't have to pace anymore . . . he'd found peace. Yoda taught me a lot about that part of the journey. I want to die like Yoda did, with my friends around me, fast, and without a lot of suffering."

Nancy shows a rare acceptance of the inevitability of her own death. In our culture death is seen as an enemy that must be kept at bay for as long as possible. Animals may not have this false belief. They may not like dying itself, but it may be that they accept death. For the time being, veterinary medicine is more pragmatic about death, although this realism may be lost as the practice takes on more of the capabilities of human medicine.

Knowing when the moment is right is a matter of listening to the dog, understanding its readiness. While Natasa was away at university, the family dog came down with *myasthenia gravis*, a condition where the nerve impulses don't travel properly. In a matter of two weeks Leica went from running on the beach to having frequent spasms and dropping to the floor. "One night she went upstairs to my parent's bedroom and woke my dad," Natasa said. "He took her outside and she went into the vegetable garden and lay down. She'd never come into the bedroom or lay down in the garden before. My dad figured that was her way of saying, 'I've lived my life, let me go.'"

Jessie, Lynn Vaughan's dog, had what was probably lupus (the diagnosis was never confirmed). Lynn and a team of veterinarians struggled for two years trying to help Jessie regain her health. Finally, her kidneys began failing. "I knew I had to make a decision about when to euthanize. I didn't believe she would want to suffer an agonizing death but I wasn't sure when the right time would be." Some blood tests were taken; the results would be available the next day. "That night, the rest of my animals—three dogs and two cats—came into the room where Jessie was sleeping and lay in a circle around her all night. I didn't sleep, I just watched them. In the morning, each animal went to Jessie to say good-bye: each in turn touched noses with her, then left the room. This was the beginning of my realizing the time had arrived." Lynn took Jessie to the vet for the test results. "I was lying with her in the back of my truck in the clinic parking lot, waiting. I remember very clearly that she lay there on her side very peacefully, facing me, and I dozed off. Suddenly I felt her paw on my cheek. I opened my eyes and she was looking at me. I knew she was saying it was time." The test results showed that Jessie was worsening fast and provided the third confirmation Lynn needed in making her decision.

As often happens, Jim and Heidi's dog Muffin went through cycles of ailing and getting better, and ailing again. After a while it became clear that he was very ill, "looking sadder and sadder. We kept him around much longer than we should have. He went really fast, but it was the hardest thing that I think either of us has ever done—to let him go. At the clinic, before the procedure itself, they let us hold him while they gave him a sedative. I offered him some pieces of chicken my mother had prepared, but he didn't really want it. He just got very sleepy. The doctor came in and said it was time. We went back into the operating room where the vet had the operating table padded with a terry cloth over it to make it soft. She put the needle into his front paw and stood there for a while, I don't know for how long. I asked, 'How long?' because every fiber of my being wanted to say, 'Stop!' 'He's gone,' she told me. The doctor let us stay there for while and be with him. I just cried. She had known Muffin most of his life and said, 'I know how hard it is, but one thing to keep in mind is that there aren't many people who get to have that beautiful a death—painless and surrounded by people who adore them.' That has helped as the years passed."

Having owned a kennel for thirty years, Honey has a wide range of experiences with many dogs and their deaths. "My dogs have definitely helped me decide," she said. "Lisa was thirteen years old and things were starting to go wrong. I was going to have to put her down, but I didn't. I came home from a trip and found her asleep on the kitchen floor. She just looked up at me and her eyes were telling me, 'Honey, I can't do this any longer. You have to do it right now.' I looked at her and thought, 'Oh God, you're right, Lisa.' I picked up the phone, called my vet, and told him I'd be there in twenty minutes." After Lisa was gone Honey cried for three days. When another of her dogs, George, had bone cancer in his mouth, and his jaw was starting to swell, Honey took four days off from work. "I looked at him and I said, 'You know, I feel really bad, George, but could you give me the next four days and I'll be with you the whole time.' And he wagged his tail. We had the four days together and we had a great time. I took him in on the fifth day. That was over ten years ago, and it still hurts."

"A customer had a Poodle who grew very old," Nancy Han began. "He was nineteen—really old for a dog—and very thin, just bones covered with skin. When she finally made the decision to put him to sleep, she asked my husband, a vet, if he would come to her house to do it. We went over together. Before that I just couldn't deal with death. The thought of people in mourning or being around something that died—it just traumatized me. Yet that experience was enlightening, because the dog was so old and so ready to leave. My thinking changed: death became part of the life cycle. The dog couldn't walk or see or hear, and he wasn't eating. He was still alive but had no substance to him—he just wasn't there anymore. He was ready to pass on. You can't backtrack—you get old and you have to move on to whatever the next step is. It was so clear and the owner was so clear. Even though it was very sad because she had to say good-bye, that wasn't all there was."

Nancy remembered a similar experience of her husband's. "He had a dog he had to put to sleep. As a veterinarian he had doctored this dog way past the usual . . . the dog had cancer. The day he made the decision, he came home and said, 'You know, Nancy, every day I tell people that I understand the reason they have to do this.' Big tears were streaming down his cheek. 'But you know, it wasn't until today that I really understood.' Somebody who has to do those things needs to feel it in order to be able to help others."

All these people who have let themselves re-experience their dogs' last days make it clear that the better we listen to our dogs, the more likely we will know if and when the time has come to make an end for them. Professionals advised

them, family and friends supported them, and, however re-
luctantly, they realized it themselves. Making that decision
their own, accepting the weight of it rather than struggling
against it or denying it, allowed them to experience their loss
without regretting the decision itself.

Natural endings

Knowing our dogs well, we can know the signs, however
minute, that indicate they still enjoy life: a wag of the tail, a
smile, a happy sigh, a leg going up for a scratch on the belly, a
snort of pleasure at a good scent. In the best of circumstances,
in the absence of pain, a dog can pass away naturally.

At thirteen, Bear came down with stomach cancer. David
and Bill decided not to put her through surgery and chemotherapy. "She lived six weeks past when the vet thought she'd
be gone. We'd thought about putting her to sleep but the idea
of taking her to the vet wasn't appealing. We made an appointment with someone who comes to the home to
euthanize. The time came around, and, well . . . she was still
alive and functioning and alert, although not very strong. So
we canceled." On Thanksgiving eve, David came home from
work to find that Bear had left her blanket. "Bill found her
under the shrubbery digging holes, in her feeble manner.
She'd never done that—my garden is precious and I trained
her not to dig in it. She looked tense and rumpled from digging around. We brushed her off and took her inside. Her
breathing was really shallow, and she was panting a little bit.

We held her and petted her, and she just passed away. She gave a little jerk and stopped breathing." David and Bill had Bear cremated but couldn't decide what to do with the ashes. Sadly, a few years later, Bill passed away, too. Then an idea came to David. "I mixed both their ashes together and planted trees out in the backyard, a dawn redwood and a mimosa that have Bear and Bill as fertilizer. The Bear and Bill trees."

As do most dog people, Stacey believes that euthanasia is important because dogs don't deserve to suffer. However, judging the quality of life isn't a black and white issue. "For example," she posits, "should the able-bodied consider people in wheelchairs as having such decreased quality of life they are candidates for euthanasia? I think not!" Stacey's dog Sara was diagnosed with spleen cancer; shortly afterward, she also lost most of her vision. "I'd thought that when Sara couldn't chase a ball, that would be the time. But her tail rarely stopped wagging, even when she was ill at the last. She always welcomed me, in spite of her infirmities. When I came home at midday to see her, she was often on the porch sleeping. Not wanting to disturb her, I would quietly slide open the door and go in. Although she was almost blind and deaf, she'd manage to find me at the other end of the house." Stacey's perspective changed and her standard for judging her dog's contentment with life lowered when she actually experienced Sara's decline and realized Sara was still enjoying life. A friend with an Irish Water Spaniel went through this period, too, lowering her standards as her dog deteriorated. Others, unaware of the nuances involved, thought she needed to put the dog down. "But we need to understand that dogs have good days and bad days, and take note of when there are more good than bad."

Inevitably, Sara's decline advanced. "I found it very difficult, watching her stumble into things. It broke my heart. I told myself, 'This is something I can handle, God says I can handle this. I'm used to working with blind or visually impaired people, I can handle this.' For a while I was so much her caretaker that I felt a little resentful—and I felt bad about that, too."

Then, one Tuesday in November, Stacey came home and found Sara underneath the stairs. "She came out," Stacey said, "even though she didn't want to, and I realized that I had very little time. She went out, took care of business and lay on the cement in the patio where it was cooler and felt better. I'm not really a religious person—I was raised Catholic and went to church on Sunday—but I am spiritual. I looked up at the clear night sky full of stars and I asked God to please take her." After a while, Stacey brought Sara in and went to bed. "Right at the stroke of three A.M., something woke me up. I thought it was my other dog, Phoebe, because she sleeps next to my bed. I looked down, but she was sound asleep. I felt drawn to check on Sara. Something called me to be with her. She was lying where I'd left her, but her head was turned in a way that wasn't natural. Her breathing was shallow and she was dying. I went to wake up Andrew, hoping I wasn't overreacting. He got up and said maybe she was sleeping really soundly, but I still thought she was dying. Andrew moved her head to a normal position, but she turned it back to open up her airway. She was going so peacefully, so acceptingly, so very gracefully. I leaned down and kissed her and told her that I loved her. I felt very calm and accepting. At three ten A.M. she took her last breath. I couldn't breathe. That was it."

The death of an old dog is good. Unburdened by imagination or by the fearful anticipation of that which cannot be known because it has never been experienced, dogs accept the approach of their passing in the way they have accepted most of what has come their way: with grace.

Mourning and acceptance

They are not dead who live
In hearts they leave behind.

Hugh Robert Orr

Each of us grieves in our own way for the passing of a beloved being: briefly or at length, alone or with others, demonstratively or silently. The grief we experience, however, is a universal feeling. Speaking of Sara's passing, Stacey said, "Even last night I dreamt about it. It's cathartic to talk about her and clarify how much she meant to me. I think the purest pain is when you lose someone you love—a person or a dog, I don't care which. Someone that was in your life every day. There are levels you have to go through in mourning. A week ago I had a dream—I could smell her, I could feel her, and I woke up at three-thirty A.M., the time of night she died six weeks ago. I sobbed as though she had just died. I'm doing well with regard to the mourning process, but it's very hard."

Sometimes the feelings of grief do not show up until much later. While Diana was living overseas, her dog Baggins was put down. "When my parents phoned to tell me I couldn't really feel anything about it. He'd suffered a couple of strokes and was having trouble breathing, so they put him to sleep. I was prepared for it because he was pretty old when I left." A year after Baggins died, Diana returned and, while staying with her parents, had to take her sister's dog to the vet for a checkup. "An older couple in the waiting room had come in to have their dog put down. I was trying hard not to cry, because it made me think of Baggins and how he'd been put to sleep. Until then, I'd never cried for him, and all of a sudden, there I was in a waiting room, crying so hard. People wondered what the hell was up with me. But it hit me then and there."

After Muffin's death, Heidi grieved deeply and fully. "I don't think I went to sleep dry-eyed for well over a month, and always woke up thinking about him," she remembered. "It was just awful, horrendous. I couldn't understand why the sun still rose. But the strangest thing happened. I woke up in that kind of twilight space after you wake up in the middle of the night, with an image of Muffin on a beach in Hawaii, wearing a Hawaiian shirt with really loud colors, sunglasses, playing a boom box, holding a mai-tai in his hand, and trying to pick up babes. I woke up howling with laughter. I knew he was okay." Whether mourning follows immediately after a dog's passing or is delayed, the grief must be experienced and worked through. Such mourning is the precursor to a life-affirming acceptance.

CHAPTER THIRTEEN

NEW BEGINNINGS

In a short space the generations of living creatures are
changed and like runners hand on the torch of life.

Lucretius

After losing a dog, we may swear off them for life—the loss is too hard, too painful. But the dog that passed away was once a puppy, and all the puppies now alive will grow old and die. The cycle continues and we are part of it. New life beckons, honoring the life past.

Just around the corner

For all of her life, Nancy Duff has been around family dogs, but Yoda was the first companion of her very own. Losing him after sixteen years was devastating. Yoda was so special for Nancy that she is apprehensive about getting another dog. "Perhaps Yoda was a 'once-in-a-lifetime' dog. I hope that's not the case—but if it is, it's nice to have had it once rather than not at all. It's hard because you do outlive your animals— that's just part of the deal." Nancy is sure she'll see some little dog and fall in love with it. "I'm definitely ready for adoption, but I don't know who will show up. I know what an intimate journey it is to have a dog—it's not a light thing."

Melissa got a dog from the pound and named her Happy after a joyful dog she'd known. Forty-six days later Happy had to be put down after coming down with distemper. "I got to hold Happy and tell her everything I wanted to say, and called her all her nicknames, and thanked her for being a part of my life . . . and then had to let her go. It's amazing how a dog can latch onto your life, even in forty-six days. Happy was my first dog out of college and I told myself there was no way I was ever going to go through that again." But a friend suggested she get another dog right away. "I told her I had to wait at least three weeks for the distemper to clear from the air. She said okay, but she had a dog I had to meet; a couple who lived across the street from her weren't caring for it. They were in the middle of breaking up and my friend saw this 'cutest dog in the whole world' sitting on the doorstep, fending for herself." That was Ttaka. "We had a couple of lunch dates, and I took her—once the air had cleared of the distemper—on the weekend of Friday the Thirteenth. And never let her go."

Melissa's temperament allowed her to accept another dog immediately after Happy's death. Other people need more time, as Barbara did. After her dog died while she was in college she felt that "a big part of my life was missing. But I wasn't ready to go out and replace that dog in a couple of days. It would have been like getting married again right after losing a husband. I needed a grieving period to get over it, and then to move on."

When a dog died, Heidi's mother told her, "'The king is dead, long live the king.' My mother's philosophy is that you go out the next day and get another dog," Heidi remembered. "That's not my philosophy. Mine is that I need to work through my grief. We had lots of people suggesting dogs to us after Muffin died, but we said no." Then Heidi had her dream of Muffin in sunglasses lounging on a tropical beach, saying hi to all the babes. Her husband Jim continued, "We decided we really should get another dog, and looked at puppies that were friendly, cute and all that, but they were just dogs. Then we went to a breeder's home to see some Scotties. As the front door opened, out came the momma Scottie and this little black ball of fur, running pell-mell toward us. She jumped in my arms and gave me a kiss. I told Heidi to write out the check. That was Amanda—we're sure that Muffin sent her to us."

Sometimes many years are needed before old wounds heal enough to try again with a new pet. Cathy remembers treating her dogs badly in her early twenties when life pressures became unbearable. "Twice I abandoned animals—just took off, leaving one dog with a friend and the other at the pound," Cathy admitted. "I deeply regretted my desperate and irresponsible actions toward my dogs, and for twenty years I didn't trust myself to make a commitment." A friend who was leaving town asked Cathy and her husband Richard to adopt her cat. It was Cathy's first pet after her long penance, but not her last. "We moved into a house on forty-two acres with abandoned dog runs calling for occupants. Then we began acquiring animals: a duck, a bunny, chickens, more ducks, more chickens, geese. I was enjoying them but I wanted the warmth and uproariousness a dog can bring. We interviewed a dozen dogs at the pound, adoptions services, and through ads. I couldn't believe the number of badly behaved dogs out there. I was about to give up when I called about an ad for miniature donkeys. The woman asked me which ad I'd responded to, and I asked what else she was selling. When she said she had a dog they were trying to find a home for, I practically jumped on her through the phone lines. I didn't know what a Springer Spaniel looked like, but made an appointment anyway. I saw Gus as soon as we got there. It was love at first sight."

But some of us must accept that there can be no next dog. Hap and Bonnie's mother retired from the ranch where Bonnie first encountered the magical connection between human and working dog. They moved to Stockton, California, where Hap had grown up, to manage apartments. "Gradually, the cattle dogs died off," Bonnie said. Then her mother got a Dachshund. "Hap had that same rapport with this miniature Dachshund that was smaller than his hand as he had with his cattle dogs. When he went out in the morning there was Missy, just a little thing, right behind this rancher still wearing his cowboy boots, checking out the property—only now it was apartments instead of rangeland." When Hap fell ill, Missy was his constant companion until he died. "Missy was always in his lap, always sitting with him. My mother won't have dogs now. We've pleaded with her, but she says she can't stand the pain when they die. So we've just had to honor that."

Easing the transition

Having a pack of dogs—or at least two!—ensures that a dog lover is never dogless. "At the time Leica passed away, we had another dog who was just a year old," Natasa explained. "Having another dog made it easier. Especially if you grew up having a dog around, you get used to a dog being under your feet. Or in the kitchen when you're cooking something, you turn around and there's a dog. It feels empty to have no one there."

Rob agrees, looking back on his succession of dogs: Skippy, Sheba, and Katie. "I've always had a 'rollover' dog, their lives overlapping. Sheba became my dog a few years before my childhood dog Skippy died. I hiked in mountain country with them both. Then I'd had Sheba about nine years when my mom died and her dog, Katie, inherited me. Now that Sheba's gone, I see things about Katie that I never really saw before. Sheba was like a partner. Katie is a buddy, a spoiled child, almost. I've enjoyed the years with just the two of us because I've gotten to know her little quirks and details of her personality. Since Katie's thirteen, I know I'll lose her some time soon. It's a fact of life. I think about not getting another dog, although I can't imagine my life without one. I just wouldn't be the same person." Rob enjoys discovering how the personalities of his dogs differ, and how different aspects emerge during the interval when there's only one.

Some people who want a dog around all the time have worked things out to ensure that they always do. Chris Zink, a veterinarian on faculty at a medical school, has perfected the art of the rollover dog. "I get a dog every five years," she said. "I know I can care properly for a maximum of three dogs. It's my lifestyle, and I really want to spend time with my dogs. I also don't want to experience having two die in a row, so I make sure I don't have them too close together. Every five years is about right, because I always have a youngster, a middle-aged one, and an older one. The best thing that you can have when one dies is another one right there. Obviously no two dogs are alike, but I believe it's the best cure for the heartbreak of losing a friend."

As Chris makes clear, we love each dog we know for its unique self. Yet taking in a new dog marks the renewal of a cycle, which did not end with the death of the old dog any more than it begins with the new. We may intuit that each dog is a variation on an archetypal pattern, thereby connecting our experience of renewal with the timelessness of the cycle.

CHAPTER FOURTEEN

TRANSFORMATIONS

If a man lived up to the reputation of a dog,
he would be a saint.

Zanzibarian proverb

Epiphanies abound for people who live with a dog. Perhaps a flash of insight tips into place the last piece of a puzzle that had been bothersomely incomplete. We make a connection between a dog's behavior and our own: annoyingly, he never sits until I say sit for the third time, but I *always* say sit three times. Suddenly, I realize I've inadvertently trained him to sit only after I issue the third command! The behavior that's been annoying me is my own doing. I see the link between what each of us does and now I can act differently to change the situation. I realize that I also repeat myself unnecessarily when speaking to *people*, explaining finally why they sometimes have seemed annoyed with me. Now I have a chance to do something about that as well.

On other, rarer occasions an insight goes deeper, touches more than a single aspect of one's personality, involving instead the whole of one's system of values. A life is changed profoundly, and will never be the same again.

Loving fully and fearlessly

Chris, the veterinarian on the faculty of Johns Hopkins University School of Medicine, is also the author of *Peak Performance,* a book on canine sports medicine and understanding dogs as athletes. Although she had always loved dogs, her involvement in obedience trials and canine performance further deepened her understanding of a dog's world and changed her view of her life's work. "When I got to veterinary school I was surprised by two things. First, I got the impression from professors that being a farm animal vet was a much higher goal than being a pet vet. Second, I came to believe that for a veterinarian dealing with people who were deeply involved with dogs would be a hassle. I was quite influenced by my professors so when I graduated I went into a large animal practice where even so, 10 percent of my work was with dogs. I found it discouraging always to be working with sick dogs, trying to treat dogs that were terminally ill and then having to euthanize them. I have a deep respect for veterinarians who have been in practice for longer than five years—they must have incredible strength to be able to endure so much that is discouraging." In her practice driving from farm to farm, Chris was frequently attacked or frightened by dogs who were territorially aggressive. "A dog would jump out from behind a barn or shrub and I had seconds to get back to the truck or it was curtains. I was bitten and chased more than once. After two years, although I loved my own dog very much, I actually disliked and feared most other dogs."

Chris began to develop an interest in canine performance events, finding that there, too, her biases were in operation. "I would look at other people's dogs and think 'Who could stand a dog that drools that much?' or 'Who would want a dog that size? Or a mixed-breed mutt like that?' I never insulted anyone's dog, but in my heart I felt I liked only my own—and maybe a few belonging to my friends.

"Then, within the first year of consulting on problems that affect canine performance, the most amazing transformation happened to me: I began to really see these dogs, see that a lot of them are working very hard, competing in performance events with a variety of problems they keep to themselves. I started to really appreciate them.

"Now when I do a consultation, I connect with the dog, empathize with it, with what it's like to be that dog—what its relationship is with its owner, how it likes or feels about the performance event and about competing and training. My last consultation shows how much my thoughts have changed. I evaluated two mixed-breed dogs that a woman had chosen at the pound. I saw them as incredibly beautiful, athletic, willing creatures with a nature that we very rarely see in human beings—a desire to please and to work with us as a team."

The change in Chris is exemplified by her relationship with her Golden Retriever, Bannor. Hard work and determination had brought Chris everything she wanted from life—until, with high hopes, she decided to compete for an Obedience Trial Championship with Bannor. She needed to garner a total of one hundred points at trial competitions, where taking first place in a large class might bring her only a handful of points—not an easy task. "Competition here on the East Coast is intense. I would drive six hours to a trial I thought none of my competition would go to and find that every major, full-time obedience trainer was competing—I didn't stand a snowball's chance in hell of placing first or second. At the end of three and a half years of competition, Bannor and I had collected eighty-five points."

Not only was the competition fierce, but Chris also felt increasingly frustrated by lapses in Bannor's attention. "In one exercise," she recalled, "Bannor had to retrieve a dumbbell and come sit in front of me. He would retrieve the dumbbell, but sit in front of the judge. Or, he'd bump into me. A single mistake like that and you're out of competition. I started to hate obedience and to hate training.

"I remember sitting down in the kitchen one day, looking at Bannor and thinking, 'He's such a screw-up. We could have finished this damn thing so long ago if he hadn't made so many mistakes.' I loved him dearly, but I could think only about how frustrating he was to work with, and the aggravating amount of time and money I was spending." While practicing with Bannor for a series of spring trials where she hoped to win the last fifteen points they needed, Chris realized something might be wrong with him. She set up a bar which Bannor had simply to jump over. "He went running to the jump and stopped dead in front of it, moving his head forward and backward, as if trying to focus on the bar. Was something wrong with his vision? His eyes had been checked every year of his life and had been fine so far."

She took him to a well-known research ophthalmologist from Cornell who told her that Bannor's eyes were fine. Puzzled, she thought to ask, "Is there some way you can judge whether he's focusing properly? He seems to have trouble with close-up things." The ophthalmologist's answer cleared it up. "Of course. His lenses have started to harden. The same thing happens to humans in our forties." Bannor *was* having trouble focusing on the bar.

Loving her dog, Chris knew at that moment his obedience career was over. She would never require her dog to jump over something he couldn't see clearly. As she absorbed the shock of learning that she would never fulfill her goal of acquiring an Obedience Trial Championship, that three and a half years of expense, frustration, and anguish would never pay off, a deeper realization gradually arose in her. "For most of the past three years I'd been thinking of Bannor as the dog who was wasting my time and money. But *I* was the dense one, not him. I hadn't realized how powerfully my frustration had affected our relationship. I saw now that the whole thing hadn't been about getting an Obedience Trial Championship at all; it had been about teaching me the importance of my relationship with my dog."

With the passage of time, Chris's understanding spread throughout the whole of her life like a drop of colored ink diffusing through a glass of clear water until the whole is tinted. "I still compete with my dogs—more frequently and in a wider variety of performance events than ever before. But the most amazing thing has happened—I have never, since Bannor, felt nervous in any competition. I'm having too much fun. If we do poorly, I don't beat myself over the head all the way home and think of how we wasted my day or what other people will think of me. Bannor made a big difference in how seriously I take things and how much I enjoy what I'm doing. He taught me a lesson that some people never learn during their whole life. It made me a different person."

Bannor was five when Chris began competing. Now he's twelve and she treasures every day she has with him. And recently, a surprise lay in wait for her. "Last November our club had its annual obedience trial, with a class for 'veteran dogs'—dogs over eight. I hadn't done any obedience work at all with Bannor for a year, and we hadn't competed for three years. But I entered him and when we got ready to go into the ring, I told him 'Bannor, you can do anything you want. You can go into this ring and just pee for all I care. This is your chance to have fun.' He was phenomenal. He heeled like a two-year old, won the class, and won highest-scoring dog in all the non-regular classes. We had a ball."

A life of quality

When Rob came to the recognition that despite Sheba's paralysis, she wasn't yet ready to die, he decided he would do whatever necessary to maintain the quality of her life as long as she lived. He could not foresee that he was committing himself to three years of hard work—which would blossom into an equally unexpected understanding.

Rob got Sheba fitted for a K-9 cart and learned massage to ease her discomfort. After three years of constant care—disproving the vet's early prediction that Rob would soon have to put her down—Sheba finally started to worsen one November, and Rob realized she would soon die. "I fought a battle with myself whether to euthanize her or not. I didn't want to, but I would have if I'd thought she was in pain. She had some pain only if she sat in one spot for too long; she'd make certain noises and I'd go in and change her position to make her comfortable." She had a cancer operation and then developed a gastrointestinal problem, building up gas and bloating. Rob learned how to massage her to express the gas, if he caught it early enough. "When I was sleeping, she could get really bloated and it would take a lot out of her. The vet said if anything would get her this would, because someday I wouldn't catch it and there was nothing to be done about it."

When Rob saw that Sheba was shutting down, he brought her to Lynn Vaughan to ease her discomfort. "The next day, I took Sheba to work with me as usual. She started to bloat and I sat with her. I tried and tried, but I couldn't get the gas out. She began licking my hand, the way she did when she was nervous, and she couldn't stop. I put her head in my lap and just petted her. I sat with her and felt her lick for about an hour and then I felt nothing. Her eyes closed and she died.

"There was a time when I felt there was almost nothing we couldn't do, so when Sheba died I felt like I'd failed. But there was also a part of me that was so proud of her and what she and I had done together that it surmounted any sense of failure. My vet had never seen anyone handle a crippled dog as large as Sheba. She said I might go a few weeks or a month, but eventually I'd have to put Sheba down. Dogs with long coats like Sheba's get raw spots or sores that are hard to keep clean. They get infected and before you know it, they're a mess. Several months later, the vet realized that there was more in it for me than keeping Sheba alive for a few weeks—that I was taking it very seriously. She saw how well Sheba was being taken care of—that she was clean, happy, and healthy. The vet used me as an example to other people, which I was very proud of. But I was continually humbled by the fact that a dog—about which we take so much for granted—has such drive and spirit. I think it inspired the vet, changed the way she felt about things. I know it changed me.

"If you study biology like I did, you're involved with death. Once, I volunteered at a necropsy station during hunting season—I necropsied deer that had been shot. You get kind of cold to this stuff. Before Sheba, I was very conventional. I figured when they got sick and you couldn't do anything for them—that's it!" That was Rob's outlook when he euthanized his boyhood dog, Skippy, who fell ill with a lymphoma. "I look back, and if I had known what I know now, I could have kept him comfortable. He had life in him and still wanted to live, but I wasn't open-minded enough to see it." Sheba taught him otherwise, and the transformation made a difference in Rob's care for himself.

"Shortly after Sheba died, I had a problem with my arm—it was losing sensitivity. It crept up to my shoulder and I started having nerve shudders. The doctors couldn't find anything. I was worrying about it, thinking it might be terminal." Eventually, Rob would learn that his symptoms were a recurrence of Lyme disease, which he'd had ten years earlier. In coping with his undiagnosed symptoms, he found that his experience with Sheba had changed him. "Because of Sheba I thought, 'I'm not going to sit around and mope. If whatever this is turns out to be terminal, then I'd never get back the time lost worrying.' With her, I took every day as it came, as another day we got to spend together. It's how I look at a lot of things now. Today is a new day and tomorrow doesn't exist right now. It's significant that I didn't feel that way before Sheba.

"I wouldn't say that carrying around an eighty-pound dog is what everyone should do. I think any decision people make is the right one for them, but taking care of Sheba is something I was meant to do, something I'm very proud of. I'm proud of what she did and what she went through. And that I could rise to her occasion."

Two lives renewed

Lee, the race car driver and mechanic, had always communicated very closely with the fifteen or so dogs he'd had. Nick was the only one of them who seemed almost to have the ability to speak. In time of great stress, he let Lee know what he felt about the situation.

Nick, whom we met earlier, was the half-Akita, half-Pit Bull confiscated by the pound from men who were training him to fight. It took Lee two years to retrain Nick not to be aggressive. Lee considers that life with Nick changed his own character. "He saved me from the weak link in my entire existence—my bad temper. I needed someone to show me there was another way to be. We both had been forced into something we didn't want to do. Nick had been trained to be a fighting dog and I'd been trained to be a boxer. When I was a kid, I boxed Golden Gloves, not because I wanted to, but because I had a stepfather who was much bigger than me. He'd say, 'If you don't box with those kids, you'll box with me.' My stepfather was a county sheriff whose model was John Wayne. He'd had sixty-four pro fights and won sixty of them, and was never knocked off his feet in the ring. I was raised to be a two-fisted, victorious person and was taught that backing off from a fight was the most cowardly thing a person could do. Most of these things start out with something really stupid. Once, in a parking lot, I'd been waiting a long time for a space, and this guy pulled right in before I could and gave me the finger. That really got to me. I was in the process of pummeling the guy when suddenly there was Nick. He'd gotten out of the car, came right up to me, and said, 'Stop. Don't do this. You can't do this. Don't.' It was just like that. I stopped. I realized. I came out of that trance that anger can produce. Nick and I got into the truck and drove off.

"I'd lived the first half of my life in this bizarre fashion, ready to hop out of my car screaming and yelling, ready to drag someone out of theirs and stuff their head through the windshield. Nick was a calming influence. He would say, 'Hey, stop. Look, you're ruining everything. Slow down.' He could cut me short with a look—it was the ultimate disapproval. No else has ever been able to do that to me; most people would just make me madder. No matter how deep the anger had gotten, he could break through, show me another way to go without classifying me as wrong or bad. And that if we followed that way it would be easier for both of us. I learned from Nick that there is no humiliation in backing up—you can feel good about yourself even if you turn and walk away from a challenge. And after you stop and walk away the first time, it gets a little easier every time after. In life we are involved in natural processes—we take it as it comes and let go as it goes. Harboring anger and frustration and remembering the bad parts is a pointless exercise. It's the destruction of our own personal temple—people have intrinsic value. What Nick taught me changed my life."

Brought to a feeling for all life

Some people seem to be waiting for a particular dog to enter their lives and fan a spark into a flame. Veronica grew up on the fifth floor of an apartment building in Budapest, where the family could never have a pet. She became a dog lover late in life—after having been afraid of dogs and animals until her fear disappeared of its own accord during her late thirties, long before Toby's unexpected and unbidden arrival. "It was eleven P.M.," Veronica remembered, "and my niece called to ask what she should do with a little dog that was lost, hungry, and thirsty. They had a couple of dogs and cats and her dad didn't want another. I jumped into the car and went over. It was love at first sight. He was maybe six months old and he lived with me until he died at twelve and a half."

Someone had lost the dog so Veronica put up signs and told everyone in the neighborhood. "He often sat in front of our store while I worked inside. About a month went by when one day, a woman stopped and said, 'That's my dog!' I ran out and, sure enough, Toby was happily jumping on her. I was very upset, so I went to the back of the store and sat down to compose myself. I shed tears, because I knew I would have to give him up to his rightful owner. I began mourning him." When Veronica had regained her composure, she went to invite the woman to take her dog back. But to her surprise the woman gave her the dog. "Little did I know that while I was in the back my husband had been talking to the woman. She had a little boy and was pregnant with a second child, so my husband convinced her that she didn't need this dog. I don't know how he did it, but he knew that my heart was aching. It was incredible.

"Toby was my first dog of my very own. He had a certain dignity about how he stood, an inborn charm. He was a gentleman. Toby came with me everywhere—to our shop, on trips with us. He was with me all the time. My husband loved him, too—the first dog he ever fell in love with."

The shop Veronica and her husband ran was on a pedestrian street in a neighborhood where people walk from their homes to nearby stores. "I didn't teach him tricks—I taught him safety on the street. I wanted him to feel freedom, to have freedom. Because I grew up in Hungary during the Second World War, personal freedom is so important to me that I wanted my dog to have it as well. Once he learned all about safety, I let him out in the morning and he went all over the neighborhood. He loved to run around and had complete freedom of the streets. People reported back that they saw Toby crossing a busy street. They told me how he waited at the curb with people waiting for the 'walk' signal, then walked across with them. To call him, I learned how to whistle very loud, and he'd come running from blocks away when he heard me."

When Toby was twelve and a half, he developed pancreatic cancer which is fatal and very painful. "He was very sick. The vet said he could either operate and lengthen his life by two or three months—but Toby would be in pain—or we could put him out of his misery. My girlfriend came over, my nephew came over, and I talked to my sister on the phone, and they all gave me positive input that I had to do it. That decision was the most wrenching in my whole life, but by the next day, I made it. I went with my husband and my nephew who loves dogs. When they gave him the shot I had him in my arms. He behaved with so much dignity that I can't ever forget the way he died. I tried to contain myself, so he wouldn't see me crying; he could sense so much how I felt. The vet had to tell me he was gone, because I was still hugging him. I cried for a long time.

"Toby had been the mascot of our store. After he died, so many people asked me about him that we made posters with his picture announcing that he had died and put them all around the neighborhood. Dogs can become your real friend. They accept you, they love you, they don't question anything. They are faithful.

"I'm very privileged. I came to realize how important he was to me and how important it was that I could share my life with another species. He could read my movements, and I learned how to interpret his body language. We had a contract, a person-to-person contract. Toby helped me to love and appreciate all forms of life. I had always loved nature—trees, bushes, and flowers—but I wasn't really tuned in to animal life.

"He helped to completely liberate in me this feeling for all life."

About the Authors

Henry and Mary Ellen Korman live with Chang, a fourteen-year-old Chow whose ability to accept infirmity has been a continual source of inspiration. They write articles about spiritual matters for journals, manuals, and books. Henry is a licensed architect and was formerly a professor of Design at City University of New York and at the Parsons School of Environmental Design. Mary Ellen holds a certificate in French Studies from the Sorbonne, and an M.A. in Counseling Psychology from Vermont College. They live in Berkeley, California.

Wildcat Canyon Press publishes books for the trade market that embrace such subjects as friendship, spirituality, women's issues, and home and family, all with a focus on self help and personal growth. Whether a collection of meditations or short essays or a how-to text, our books are designed to enlighten and encourage our readers' hearts and souls. While we insist on a certain intimacy in our authors' writing, we also take responsibility to ensure that their messages are accessible to readers of all levels. Great care is taken to create books that inspire reflection and improve the quality of our lives. Our books demand to be shared and are frequently given as gifts.

For a catalog of our publications, please write:

WILDCAT CANYON PRESS
2716 Ninth Street
Berkeley, California 94710
Phone: (510) 848-3600
Fax: (510) 848-1326
Circulus@aol.com
http://www.ReadersNdex.com/wildcatcanyon